TABLE OF CONTENTS

ACRONYMS

AMISOM	African Union Mission in Somalia
AU PSC	African Union Peace and Security Council
AU	African Union
CGSC	Command and General Staff College
CIA	Central Intelligence Agency
EAR	Eastern Africa Region
EU	European Union
FM	Field Manual (United States Army)
GDP	Gross Domestic Product
ICU	Islamic Courts Union
ICS	Integrated Country Strategy
IGAD	Intergovernmental Authority on Development
IMF	International Monetary Fund
ISI	Inter Service Intelligence (Government of Pakistan)
NATO	North Atlantic Treaty Organization
NSC	National Security Council (United States)
NSS	National Security Strategy (United States)
OPEC	Organization of Petroleum Exporting Countries
SNA	Somali National Army
TFG	Transitional Federal Government
TNG	Transitional National Government
UN	United Nations

UNDP	United Nations Development Program
UNESCO	United Nations Educational Scientific and Cultural Organization
UNICEF	United Nations International Children's Emergency Fund
UNISOM	United Nations in Somalia
UNITAF	Unified Task Force (to Somalia)
UNSC	United Nations Security Council
US	United States
WSLF	Western Somalia Liberation Front
WWII	World War Two

ILLUSTRATIONS

TABLES

CHAPTER 1

INTRODUCTION

The overall aim of this paper is to explore the United States policy objective of

eliminating the Al Shabaab terrorist organization. Al Shabaab, also known as the

Mujahidin Youth Movement (MYM), was formally identified as a "specially designated

global terrorist" in February of 2008 by the U.S. Government.[1] Since that time Al

Shabaab has played a prominent role in U.S. policies for the Horn of Africa and for

Somalia in particular. On 12 April 2010, with Executive Order 13536, President Obama

declared a national emergency with respect to Somalia, and on 7 April 2014 the President

extended the national emergency declaration.[2] Executive Order 13536 fingers Al Shabaab

by name as major source of destabilization, while also orienting on the deterioration of

security, continuation of violence, misappropriation of public assets (corruption), and acts

of piracy off the coast of Somalia.

Taken as a whole, Somalia is important to the U.S. for five reasons. The first

reason is a matter of geography; Somalia is in a strategically important location due to its

proximity to major international sea lines of communication as well as its location

between the Middle East and the whole of Africa. The second reason is that Somalia

continues to serve as a haven for regional maritime piracy and is consequently one of the

---

[1]Office of the Coordinator for Counterterrorism, "Designation of al-Shabaab as a Specially Designated Global Terrorist," U.S. Department of State website, 26 February 2008, http://www.state.gov/j/ct/rls/other/des/102448.htm (accessed 17 May 2014).

[2]Office of the Press Secretary, "Notice – Continuation of the National Emergency with Respect to Somalia," 7 April 2014, http://www.whitehouse.gov/the-press-office/2014/04/07/notice-continuation-national-emergency-respect-somalia (accessed 12 April 2014).

1

largest fronts for combating this problem. The third reason is that Somalia, due to more than 20 years of continuous conflict, is the origin of more than 1 million refugees worldwide, including at least 150,000 in the United States.[3] The fourth reason is that Somalia is suspected of being host to a significant volume of hydrocarbon resources within its borders.[4] While the U.S. might be able to achieve energy independence in the coming years, most trading partners of the U.S. are not on a trajectory to achieve this goal. This in turn means that the global economy as a whole (including most U.S. allies and partners) will remain fundamentally linked to hydrocarbons for the foreseeable future. The fifth reason is the presence of the terrorist organization Al Shabaab itself. As a recently anointed affiliate of Al Qaeda and as an adherent to extreme Wahhabist principles, Al Shabaab has consistently asserted itself as a destabilizing and violent entity both inside and outside of Somalia's borders.

Research Questions

Primary Research Question: Are U.S. policies towards Somalia effective?

Secondary Research Questions: How have U.S. policies for Somalia evolved over the last two decades? Over the long term, are U.S. policies for Somalia inadvertently strengthening Al Shabaab?

---

[3] Josh Richardson, "The Somali Diaspora: A Key Counterterrorism Ally," https://www.ctc.usma.edu/posts/the-somali-diaspora-a-key-counterterrorism-ally (accessed 15 April 2014).

[4] Mark Fineman, "The Oil Factor In Somalia," *Los Angeles Times*, 18 January 1993, http://articles.latimes.com/1993-01-18/news/mn-1337_1_oil-reserves (accessed 1 April 2014).

Assumptions

This study contains three principal assumptions. The first assumption is that the U.S. is interested in being the predominant power exerting influence over the Horn of Africa. The second assumption is that the international community is committed to making Somalia a stable and prosperous country. The third assumption, which is in deference to the ongoing campaigns for independence in the semi-autonomous regions of Puntland and Somaliland, is that the international community will continue to recognize Somalia's current borders.

Definitions

In most instances, definitions are included within text of this research project. However, to prevent possible misunderstanding the following three terms are defined: Horn of Africa, Terrorism, and Wahhabism.

Horn of Africa is defined as the region in eastern Africa that includes the four countries of Eritrea, Djibouti, Ethiopia, and Somalia. Though sometimes included in other Horn of Africa definitions, the nations of Kenya, Uganda, and Sudan are not included as part of region for the purposes of this paper. In the few instances where this definition conflicts with the definition used by an external source, the discrepancy is highlighted in order to prevent any possible confusion.

Terrorism is defined in accordance with the 18 U.S.C. § 2331 definition for international terrorism, which ascribes the following meaning: "Involve violent acts or acts dangerous to human life that violate federal or state law; Appear to be intended (i) to intimidate or coerce a civilian population; (ii) to influence the policy of a government by intimidation or coercion; or (iii) to affect the conduct of a government by mass

3

destruction, assassination, or kidnapping; and Occur primarily outside the territorial jurisdiction of the U.S., or transcend national boundaries in terms of the means by which they are accomplished, the persons they appear intended to intimidate or coerce, or the locale in which their perpetrators operate or seek asylum."[5]

It is important to recognize that the term terrorism has not been used consistently over the course of the last two or three decades, nor is it described consistently between all U.S. Federal Government agencies.[6] In situations where the definition specified here conflicts with the definition used by a source, the discrepancy is highlighted in order to prevent possible confusion.

Wahhabism is an ultra-orthodox sect of Sunni Islam that is "emphasized by the unity of God; seeks to return Muslims to principles and practices of the earliest days of Islam; is opposed to Sufi orders; and vigorously seeks expansion of territorial control."[7] Wahhabism was created by an eighteenth century religious reformer by the name of Abd al-Wahhab. Wahhabism is promoted and practiced by several Islamic terrorist organizations including Al Qaeda, Al Shabaab, and the Taliban. Wahhabism is not synonymous with terrorism and is associated with many non-terrorist entities such as the government of Saudi Arabia. Due in large part to its Sunni foundation, Wahhabism is incompatible with Shia based organizations like the Islamic Republic of Iran and

---

[5]U.S. Government, Definitions of Terrorism in the U.S. Code, U.S. Government, http://www.fbi.gov/about-us/investigate/terrorism/terrorism-definition (accessed 16 May 2014).

[6]Brian Whitaker, "The definition of terrorism," *The Guardian*, 7 May 2001, http://www.theguardian.com/world/2001/may/07/terrorism (accessed 15 May 2014).

[7]Sydney Nettleton Fisher and William Ochsenwald, *The Middle East: A History* Vol II (New York: McGraw-Hill, 1997), 266.

Hizballah. Wahhabism is sometimes used by authors interchangeably with the term Salafism. However, the two terms and the movements associated with them have different roots and should not be viewed as synonymous. Consequently, the terms Salaf, Salafi, Salafist, Salafism, and Salafiyyun are avoided in this paper. For a detailed description regarding the difference between the two terms, please see *The Islamic Traditions of Wahhabism and Salafiyya* by the Congressional Research Service.[8]

Limitations

This research effort adopts three primary limitations. The first limitation is in regards to the significance of tribes (or clans) in Somalia. The second limitation is in regards to ongoing international struggle with piracy in the vicinity of Somalia. The third limitation orients on the balance of depth and breadth in the study as a whole.

Though of meaningful significance, this study does not focus heavily on the importance of tribal affiliation in Somalia. Clan relations and affiliations do not contain the same potential for volatility in Somalia as they often achieve elsewhere in Africa. All of the principal clans in Somalia claim the same common Arab root and share common culture, ethnicity, language, and religion. This commonality is generally not shared in other parts of Africa where clans sometimes adopt significantly different profiles from each other and in turn fight and persecute each other. This is not to say that Somalis do not persecute and fight each other, rather the aim here is to observe that the Somali conflict is usually (though not always) rooted in non-clan based motivations. For an

---

[8]Christopher M. Blanchard, *The Islamic Traditions of Wahhabism and Salafiyya* (Washington, DC: CRS Report for Congress, 2007).

excellent yet reasonably concise study on Somali clans, readers should seek the Civil-Military Fusion Center's paper on clan structure in Somalia.

Additionally, this study excludes any direct consideration of maritime piracy which has been studied in great depth by other authors. While Al Shabaab may be involved in piracy at least in a tacit way, it is not a principal end state aim of the organization. Numerous studies regarding Somalia and piracy have been accomplished by defense professionals at the U.S. Naval Post Graduate School as well as by students at the U.S. Naval War College.

Finally, this project seeks to strike a meaningful balance between depth and breadth of research with an ultimate aim of providing a previously unconsidered insight into the ongoing problems in Somalia with respect to the terrorist organization Al Shabaab. Greater depth could have been achieved in each category of research, but this would have been at the expense of increased breadth of the overall project. Conversely, greater breadth could have been accomplished at the expense of depth.

Organization of the Study

This research paper is divided into five chapters. The first chapter serves as the introduction and provides the setting and context for the study. The second chapter contains the literature review. The third chapter outlines research methodology adopted for this project. Chapter four presents the results of the research. Finally, chapter five provides conclusions and recommendations.

Figure 1.   Map of Somalia with Officially Recognized Administrative Districts

Source: United Nations Department of Field Support, Cartographic Section, "Map of Somalia," December 2011, http://www.un.org/depts/Cartographic/map/profile/somalia.pdf (accessed 2 May 2014).

CHAPTER 2

Er…no Sir, we don't seem to have anything on Somalia
                    Bookkeeper at the World Bank's Development
                    Book Store (April 2014)

Introduction

Though several books, articles, webpages, and the like, have been published with

respect to the study of both Somalia and Al Shabaab, the volume of overall publications

is relatively low by comparison with similar entities. On amazon.com's book page, a

word search for Somalia came up 3,627 times, while searches for Ethiopia came up 9,455

times. In a similar vein, word searches for the Sudan came up 9,095 times and searches

for Kenya yielded 17,622 results. Additionally, an in person visit to the World Bank's

highly respected Development Book Store (The InfoShop – The World Bank; located on

the corner of Pennsylvania and 18th streets in Washington D.C. . . . a mere block from

the White House), which specializes in stocking both general, regional, and country

specific publications on international development, yielded not a single volume on

Somalia. That said, direct study of the quantity, availability, and readership of

publications regarding Somalia is not a focus of this paper and the aforementioned

statistics should only be considered in an anecdotal light at most. What is important is

that sufficient information regarding both Somalia and the terrorist organization Al

Shabaab exists to support the intended scope of research for this project.

This chapter provides a concise summary of principal literature sources relevant

to this study and is organized into five parts. The initial element of the chapter serves as

the introduction and guide. The second part provides a summary of information directly relevant to Somalia as a whole. The third portion of the chapter provides a summary for recent literature regarding Al Shabaab. The fourth portion of the chapter orients on prominent theories for eliminating terrorist organizations. The final portion of the chapter orients on prominent international development methods.

Somalia

With respect to the direct study of Somalia and the relevant application of U.S. policy, U.S. federal government sources of information have been among the most useful to this study. The U.S. Department of State's *Integrated Country Strategy (ICS) for Somalia, FY 14-17* provided insight regarding the U.S. view of Somalia and how the U.S. sees itself interacting with the nation and its problems in the near future. This document's principal thrust is in respect to the diplomatic instrument of national power. However, it also allows for important insight into all four elements of national power with respect to Somalia. The Congressional Research Service (CRS) has also provided multiple excellent products with respect to Somalia. The CRS Reports for Congress have been especially useful in their ability to provide a current (as of the date of each publication) macro view of the situation in Somalia while also outlining the behaviors of external players like the African Union, the European Union, and China. Additional U.S. federal government sources include U.S. Agency for International Development (USAID) annual reports that provide excellent information regarding the breadth and depth of U.S. funding across the Horn of Africa.

In *Somalia: State Collapse and the Threat of Terrorism*, Ken Menkhaus identifies that, following the Somali governmental collapse in 1991 and through to 2004, Somalia has been run by clans. He asserts, prior to the emergence of the Islamic Courts Union, that clans constituted the main form of protection for individuals and the Somali society. Additionally, he highlights the rapidly growing popular support for Islamists and the application of sharia law through an organized system of courts. The clan-based customary law system "xeer" appears to have lost ground throughout Somalia to sharia law. Menkhaus further highlights emerging geographic and political partitions within Somalia; the three regions being Somaliland, Puntland, and South-Central Somalia. He considers the latter, which is home to the more radical of the Islamists, to be by far the most dangerous. Menkaus also takes time in his book to review the travesty of the overall socio-economic and humanitarian situation. However, he observes that many of the Somali do not feel motivated to change the current situation in Somalia and are comfortable maneuvering within the current situation. Menkaus feels that the time is not yet ripe for the international community to stand up a new government in Somalia. Instead he argues that the international community should focus on funneling support to and through the existing pockets of stability presently within Somalia.

Al Shabaab

As with Somalia, U.S. federal government publications regarding Al Shabaab have also been especially useful. In particular, The CRS Report for Congress titled: *Countering Terrorism in East Africa: The U.S. Response* by Lauren Ploch provides a meaningful summary of Al Shabaab and U.S. interaction through the middle of 2010.

In *After bin Laden: Al Qaeda, the Next Generation,* Abdel Bari Atwan details Al Qaeda's recent evolutionary transitions. Al Qaeda has spread its wings farther afield and has become more decentralized since the 11 September 2001 terrorist attacks. Part of Al Qaeda's recent transition includes engagement with like-minded organizations in the

Horn of Africa among several other places. That Al Shabaab has joined Al Qaeda as an affiliate organization is no surprise to Atwan.

In *Somalia: Line in the Sand–Identification of MYM Vulnerabilities*, Wells and Cuevas of the U.S. Army War College–Center For Strategic Leadership outline the strengths and weaknesses of the Al Shabaab terrorist organization (as of 2011). They make particular note of Al Shabaab's excellent advantage in information operations within Somalia and the surrounding region. The authors also review the national instruments of power (diplomatic, information, military, economic) with respect to Al Shabaab.

In *Islamism and its Enemies in the Horn of Africa,* Alex de Waal discusses the foundations of conservative Islam in the Horn of Africa. De Waal links the spread of conservative Islam in the region principally to the Muslim Brotherhood in Egypt but also to Saudi Arabia's Wahhabist-oriented government. The author makes an important discovery in identifying that "Islamists" have been successful in providing governance (or least something passing for governance) in failed states. He also asserts that success has been due in part to the stable organizational structure of religious leaders who are able to provide some level of consistency regarding basic services such as administration of justice and facilitation of commerce. Additionally, de Waal observes that Islamists have achieved success in part by working with, and not against, militarized clans within the Horn of Africa.

The African Jihad: Bin Laden's Quest for the Horn of Africa by Gregory A. Pirio describes the evolution of radical Islamic groups in the Horn of Africa. Pirio begins his book in the early 1990s by describing the efforts of Osama Bin Laden and Al Qaeda, who were located in Sudan, to establish Islamic hegemony in the Horn of Africa. The author describes the integrated relationships between Al Qaeda, bin Laden, and the principal radical Islamic movements across the Horn of Africa from the early 1990s through to the establishment of the Islamic Courts Union (ICU) in Somalia. Pirio clearly traces the linkages between Al Qaeda and the emergence of the ICU in Somalia. Though the book was published in 2007 and before the emergence of Al Shabaab on the international level, Pirio has enabled the view of a connection between Al Shabaab (which was created from within the ICU) and Al Qaeda. If de Waal is to be believed, then the recent affiliation between Al Shabaab and Al Qaeda should not be seen as a new development, but instead as a reunification of close relatives.

Theories on Eliminating Terrorist Organizations

The most important source has been RAND Corporation's excellent quantitative study titled *How Terrorist Groups End; Lessons for Countering al Qa'ida*. This quantitative study published in 2008 provides analysis of 648 terrorist organizations during the latter half of the twentieth century.

Counterinsurgency Warfare; Theory and Practice, which was originally published in 1964 by David Galula, is considered by many to be the most important counterinsurgency text written during the twentieth century. Galula, a French veteran of several conflicts spanning three continents, argues that the key to controlling (ending) insurgency is to first control the general population. Galula is 'hearts and minds' oriented and offers a road map to would-be counterinsurgents on how to eliminate insurgencies. He argues that successful counterinsurgencies employ three concepts. The first is that the counterinsurgents should be assembled as one organization (unity of command) in order to prevent confusion and discord. The second concept is that that the overall counterinsurgent strategy should focus on the least contested regions first before moving into more contested areas. The third concept is to adopt a patient phased-approach to rooting out insurgents. Success is achieved when the overall population rejects the insurgents because it has been convinced that the counterinsurgents will ultimately prevail.

How Terrorism Ends by Audrey Kurth Cronin can in some ways be viewed as the qualitative version of RAND's quantitatively based *How Terrorist Groups End; Lessons for Countering al Qa'ida.* Cronin invokes echoes of the Clausewitzian trinity with her characterization of terrorist campaigns as being a "triad" of three participants: the group, the government, and the audience.[9] She also identifies patterns that have upended terrorist organizations and then highlights the patterns through a series of case studies. The patterns are: decapitation (removing the leader), negotiation (reconciling the group into legitimacy), success (the terrorists win), failure (the group disintegrates), repression (destruction by force), and reorientation (transitioning to conventional warfare). However, Cronin observes that "the end of terrorism is not necessarily the beginning of peace."[10]

The *National Strategy for Combating Terrorism* (June 2011) by the United States Government is an important document which at least nominally represents itself as providing a macro view of the U.S. strategy for confronting terrorism. Unfortunately, the

---

[9]Note: Carl Von Clausewitz first coined the phrase 'remarkable trinity' which includes the dynamic between the citizens, the government, and the military.

[10]Audrey Kurth Cronin, *How Terrorism Ends: Understanding the Decline and Demise of Terrorist Campaigns* (Princeton, NJ: Princeton University Press, 2009), 146.

document is somewhat vague regarding the application of U.S. national instruments of power. However, the document does provide clear descriptions of perceived threats to U.S. interests with respect to terrorism. Specifically, the document identifies ten areas of focus at the strategic level:

1. The Homeland

2. South Asia: Al-Qa'ida and its Affiliates and Adherents

3. Arabian Peninsula: Al-Qa'ida and Al-Qa'ida in the Arabian Peninsula (AQAP)

4. East Africa: Al-Qa'ida in East Africa and Al-Shabaab

5. Europe

6. Iraq: Al-Qa'ida in Iraq (AQI)

7. Maghreb and Sahel: Al-Qa'ida in the Lands of the Islamic Maghreb (AQIM)

8. Southeast Asia: Al-Qa'ida and its Affiliates and Adherents

9. Central Asia: Al-Qa'ida and its Affiliates and Adherents

10. Information and Ideas: Al-Qa'ida Ideology, Messaging, and Resonance

Aside from Al Qaeda (Al Qa'ida) itself or a direct Al Qaeda affiliate, Al Shabaab is the only terrorist organization earning its own area of focus in the U.S. *National Strategy for Combating Terrorism* which underscores the perceived threat posed by Al Shabaab. Additionally the document indicates that the U.S. is concerned that Al Shabaab may soon seek to strike, not only outside of the borders of Somalia, but also outside of the region.

The U.S. Army's Field Manual (FM) 3-24 *Counterterrorism* provides the U.S. Army's formalized doctrine on how to upend insurgencies and serves as an operational and tactical companion to the strategic view provided in the *National Strategy for*

Combating Terrorism. The FM provides suggested approaches and in some cases formulas for operational and tactical leaders to consider during before and during the conduct of counterinsurgency operations. The FM frequently observes that every insurgency is different and that the methods the document should be adapted dynamically to each unique situation.

Theories on International Development Methods

In *Development Theory*, Jan Naederveen Pieterse provides a seemingly comprehensive guide to the current state of development theory. His book outlines both opposing and supporting development theories and offers sophisticated conjecture on the way ahead for the international development community. In his latest edition, Pieterse identifies four overarching theories in development and organizes them by the period in time in which they each respectively represented the vanguard. The periods being the prelude to development and catch up polices (1800s to 1950), postwar Keynesian consensus (1950 to 1980), the neoliberal era of the Washington consensus (1980-2000), and new 'post Washington consensus era' which Pieterse has declined to ascribe a name to due to its rapidly evolving state: "So far we know that neoliberalism is passé and the Washington consensus is no more; we know there are trend breaks and new trends, but it may be too early as yet to discern a new pattern."[11] Pieterse argues that a large part of the ongoing evolution in development theory has been driven by economic instability of the U.S. which has in turn translated to instability across the world. "American capitalism has gone from crisis to crisis, with the management of each crisis precipitating the next. The

---

[11]Jan Nederveen Pieterse, *Development Theory,* 2nd ed. (London: Sage Publications, 2010), Preface.

crescendo of crises demonstrates the downside of neoliberalism, the flipside of deregulation."[12] Additionally, Pieterse argues that American geo political hegemony is continuing to weaken while China's power is on the rise. With respect to Somalia, the views expressed by Pieterse lead the reader to believe that leaders from developing countries (like Somalia) may perceive that they have more appealing options for international assistance than to embrace the U.S. and its approach to development.

William Easterly is far more pessimistic than many of his peers with his provocatively titled *The White Man's Burden: Why the West's Efforts to Aid the Rest Have Done So Much Ill and So Little Good*. The title seems to sum it up for Easterly, who argues that much of the effort spent trying to improve the third world is wasted effort. In particular, he is critical of western nations seeking to impose their own image on developing nations. With the background of being an MIT educated economist and as a former employee of the World Bank, Easterly has consistently projected a skeptical numbers-oriented view of western development efforts in much of his writing.

By contrast, in *The End of Poverty; Economic Possibilities For Our Time*, Jeffery Sachs argues that solving the problems of the third world is well within the grasp of the developed nations and that there is no time like the present to take care of business.

---

[12]Pieterse, *Development Theory*, 204.

CHAPTER 3

Research Methodology

In addressing the primary research question (Are U.S. policies towards Somalia effective?), research utilizes principally qualitative analysis methods. Additionally, in some supporting instances quantitative analysis methods are employed.

Research Design

This paper utilizes the qualitative research approach through the use of case studies in order to further reveal cause and effect trends in U.S. foreign policy relevant to the primary research question. Supporting quantitative research for this project involves correlational and cause-comparative analysis. Correlational quantitative analysis seeks to reveal the relationship between two or more measurable variables. Cause-comparative quantitative analysis is focused on determining a direct cause and effect relationship between variables. The research included in this project does not involve the generation of *raw* data as is typically done with descriptive and experimental quantitative research methods.

Organization

Research is divided into three main parts. The first portion of research provides qualitative and quantitative analysis regarding Al Shabaab. The second portion of research is a case study provides a qualitative comparison of U.S. policy for Somalia in contrast with U.S. policy for Afghanistan from 1981 to 2001, with an eye on the emergence of Al Shabaab and the Taliban. The third portion of research is the second case study, which focuses on a qualitative comparison of U.S. policy for Somalia in contrast with U.S. policy for Iran between 1953 and the early 1980s with the aim of revealing the subsequent emergence of Al Shabaab and Hizballah.

Qualitative

The initial portion of research provides a direct assessment of Al Shabaab's organizational profile. This aspect of the research draws its methodology from the 2008 RAND Corporation book titled *How Terrorist Groups End; Lessons for Countering al Qa'ida*.[13] The RAND study involves quantitative analysis of 648 terrorist groups between the years 1968 and 2006 and orients on measuring how terrorist groups cease to exist. RAND's analysis provides meaningful statistical analysis regarding which influencing factors contributed to the final disposition of terrorist organizations during the period studied. Of particular interest, the RAND paper identifies five major ways in which terrorist groups end; through policing, by military force, by splintering into multiple organizations, through politics, or by achieving victory and provides statistical likelihoods, relevant to the type of terrorist organization, on failure or success. The statistics are driven by analysis in the membership, funding, ideology, duration of existence, presence of an insurgency, and consideration of the Gross Domestic Product (GDP) of the host nation. Al Shabaab emerged as an independent organization after the period covered by the study. However, by gathering the relevant background information (for example: membership, funding, ideology), it is possible to cross reference the statistical momentum of the RAND effort to ascribe likelihoods to how, and if, Al Shabaab will cease to exist. Keeping in mind that ending terrorist groups, especially

---

[13]Seth G. Jones and Martin C. Libicki; *How Terrorist Groups End: Lessons for Countering Al Qa'ida* (Santa Monica, CA: RAND Corporation, 2008).

emerging trans-national ones like Al Shabaab, is ostensibly a major U.S. policy objective.[14] Figure 2 has been taken directly from the RAND study and provides a breakdown of the relatively simple but effective comparison that was applied to each of the 648 terrorist groups considered.

Figure 2.   RAND Study (MG741-2.1) Categorical Descriptions

Source: Seth G. Jones and Martin C. Libicki; *How Terrorist Groups End: Lessons for Countering Al Qa'ida* (Santa Monica, CA: RAND Corporation, 2008), 142.

This portion of the project will gather the necessary data to fill out Table 1 (emulated from the RAND study) and pulls from all 648 organizations to gain insight into the statistical propensities of Al Shabaab's organizational profile. For the purposes of this paper, the inclusion of Al Shabaab brings the overall sample size to 649 organizations.

---

[14]White House, *National Strategy for Counterterrorism* (Washington, DC: Whitehouse, June 2011), 14.

Source: Created by Author utilizing format from Seth G. Jones and Martin C. Libicki; *How Terrorist Groups End: Lessons for Countering Al Qa'ida* (Santa Monica, CA: RAND Corporation, 2008), 143.

This portion of research also includes an assessment of troop to task ratios as applied against Al Shabaab. Specifically, the available number of security force personnel present in Somalia as compared to the size of the overall population and the size of the geographic area being secured. While the U.S. does not presently have a uniformed military presence in Somalia, the growing presence of U.S. facilitated AMISOM personnel continues to play an important role in the overall security equation. This portion of the project reviews security force strength in Somalia for the last 10 years against Al Shabaab member numbers, geographic area, and overall population size (see Table 4). This information enables a comparison of the relevant troop-to-task ratios for offense and stability operations (both of which are relevant in the conflict with Al Shabaab). An insufficient troop to task ratio will lower the likelihood of achieving success against an organization with Al Shabaab's profile.

Table 2.   Method Table–Military

	2005	2006	2007	2008	2009	2010	2011	2012	2013	2014	Trend	Anticipated Trend
Authorized AMISOM Troop Strength												Steady Increase
Actual AMISOM Troop Strength												Steady Increase
Somali (TNG) Troop Strength												Steady Increase
Al Shabaab member strength												Steady Increase, then a peak followed by a decline
Geographic Area Covered												(fixed)
Overall Population Size												Modest Growth
Stability - Troop to task ratio												Improving
Offense - Troop to task ratio												Improving

Source: Created by author.

Selection of Supporting Case Studies

Of the many possible supporting case studies that might have been utilized in this study, Afghanistan-Taliban and Iran-Hizballah were selected for three reasons. The first reason is that the case studies, or rather their targets, are named in the U.S. National Security Strategy (NSS).[15] Aside from Al Qaeda, no other terrorist organization merits this level of attention from the NSS. The second reason is that Al Shabaab, Hizballah, and the Taliban all share similar profiles as terrorist organizations. All three are based on Islamic religious ideologies and are seeking to establish a style of government founded on sharia law. This is not to say that the three organizations are identical. For instance while the Taliban and Al Shabaab are Sunni and Wahhabist in their ideology, Hizballah is a Shia based organization. The Taliban and Hizballah have confined their terrorist

---

[15]White House, *National Security Strategy of the United States* (Washington, DC: Whitehouse, 2010), 4, 20, 26.

21

activities to specific geographic boundaries. By contrast Al Shabaab, though principally focused on Somalia, has demonstrated a willingness to attack targets in neighboring states. The third reason is that like Somalia, Afghanistan and Iran have been subject to dramatic transitions in U.S. policy in recent history. The review of turbulence in U.S. policy with respect to Somalia and the consequences for Al Shabaab is an important aspect of this research project. Al Qaeda was ruled out as a case study option due to its overtly international focus, wide geographic reach, and broad goals as compared to Al Shabaab.

Supporting Case Studies

The Afghanistan - Taliban case study takes a close look at the consequences of the U.S. policy approach of developing and supporting an insurgency and the transition away from that policy following the Soviet withdrawal from Afghanistan in 1989. In keeping with the NSC's 1950 NSC 68 policy directive, the U.S. pursued a policy of containment against Soviet territorial and ideological expansion across the globe. Like Afghanistan in the 1980s, the Horn of Africa was the scene of a proxy war between the U.S. and the Soviet Union in the 1970s. This case study compares the U.S. application of policy in the two wars and the U.S. approach following the wars. Specifically, research will focus on five comparative indicators; proxy conflict (motivated by NSC 68), indirect funding methods, leveraging of Islamic fundamentalist, rapid withdraw of funding following success against the Soviets, and subsequent growth of a Muslim fundamentalist movement (see Table 6). This Muslim fundamentalist movement, with its roots in Cold War era U.S. policy, evolved into the Taliban.

Table 3.   Method Table–Afghanistan Case Study

	Afghanistan	Somalia
Proxy War		
Indirect funding motivated by policy of containment		
Leveraging Muslim Fundamentalist		
Rapid pull back of funds following success against Soviets		
Subsequent Growth of Muslim Fundamentalist movement		

Source: Created by author.

The Iran - Hizballah case study takes a look at the motivations behind Operation Ajax (the 1953 U.S. and U.K. led coup to overthrow the Iranian Prime Minister) and the long term national security implications. Like Iran, both oil and natural gas have been discovered in Somalia. And like Iran, Somalia has a strong Islamic fundamentalist sentiment. This case study compares the motivations behind U.S. policy and the long term consequences. Specifically this part of the paper considers the presence of natural resources, the subsequent involvement of U.S. (or U.S. allied) natural resource corporations, U.S. facilitated manipulation of the host government, and the following emergence of Islamic fundamentalist organizations (see Table 7). The first Islamic fundamentalist organization spawned from this sequence of events was the Islamic Republic of Iran itself. In turn, former military personnel of the Islamic Republic of Iran founded Hizballah in the early 1980s. Since that time, Iran has consistently provided material support to Hizballah.

Table 4.   Method Table–Iran Case Study

	Iran	Somalia
Discovery of Natural Resources		
Subsequent Involvement of U.S. (or U.S. Allied) natural resource corporations		
Manipulation of host government		
Emergence of Islamic Fundamentalist organizations		

Source: Created by author.

Additionally, data from the RAND study for both the Taliban and Hizballah will be compared against the results of the Al Shabaab profile.

Chapter Summary

This study uses both qualitative and quantitative methods to address the primary research question. Three case studies are utilized with the aim of discerning the motivations and consequences of U.S. policy in Somalia. Additionally, research includes some quantitative analysis of U.S. policy for Al Shabaab as well as direct analysis of Al Shabaab as an organization. When taken as a whole, the research seeks to establish a connection between U.S. policies and the likelihood of successfully eliminating the Al Shabaab terrorist organization.

CHAPTER 4

Analysis Overview

This chapter provides results of the research and is divided into four sections in accordance with the methodology described in chapter three. The first portion of the chapter provides a concise overview. The second portion covers analysis of Al Shabaab. The third portion is a case study focusing on a comparison between Somalia and Afghanistan with a view to the Taliban and Al Shabaab. The fourth and final portion of this chapter includes a case study focusing on Somalia and Iran with consideration Hizballah and Al Shabaab.

Somalia and Al Shabaab

This section of analysis includes two elements. The first element provides results of the Al Shabaab profile (utilizing RAND Corporation's *How Terrorist Groups End* methodology).[16] The second element provides quantitative analysis of the African Union Mission in Somalia (AMISOM) in terms of troop to task ratios.

The Al Shabaab Profile

In accordance with the method outlined in chapter three, Figure 3 has been pulled directly from the RAND study and describes the categories by which 649 terrorist organizations have been compared. Table 5 shows the specific raw result for Al Qai'da provided in the RAND study, as well as the result for this paper with respect to Al Shabaab.

---

[16]Jones and Libicki, *How Terrorist Groups End*, 142-185.

25

Table 5.   Raw results for Al Qaeda and Al Shabaab

Source: Created by author utilizing partial data from Seth G. Jones and Martin C. Libicki; *How Terrorist Groups End: Lessons for Countering Al Qa'ida* (Santa Monica, CA: RAND Corporation, 2008), 142.

With respect to the parameters defined by the RAND study, Al Shabaab carries the same organizational profile as Al Qai'da . . . with one exception. The exception is that Al Shabaab is larger in terms of overall peak organizational size. RAND identified Al Qai'da as having a peak size at about 1,000. By contrast, Al Shabaab is typically identified as having between 4,000 and 10,000 members.[17] For the purposes of this study 5,000 has been selected as the peak number of organizational members for Al Shabaab. While it is possible that Al Shabaab has achieved higher member numbers, it is better for this project to error on the side of caution and commit to a more modest number.

---

[17]David Smith, "Al-Shabaab rebuilds forces in Somalia as African Union campaign stalls," *The Guardian*, 28 October 2013, www.theguardian.com/world/ 2013/oct/28/al-shabaab-somalia-african-union (accessed 2 March 2014).

Like Al Qai'da, Al Shabaab is principally based in a country where the average annual income of its citizens is low.[18] Indeed, Somalia's Gross National Income is in the bottom percentage of all nations (Category: L).[19] The Freedom House rankings for freedom of the press have consistently appointed Somalia the lowest possible rating of Not Free (Category: NF).[20] As discussed in chapter one, Al Shabaab is an organization driven principally by religious beliefs (Category: R). Finally Al Shabaab is committed to the goal of establishing a Caliphate *empire* (Category: E).[21] Like Al Qai'da, Al Shabaab has not ended (Category: *Null*).[22]

The RAND study carries a couple of arresting statistical observations. The study found that most terrorist groups typically end as the result of one of the two following reasons. The most common way is for the terrorist organization to transition to non-

---

[18]RAND chose Afghanistan as the Al Qaeda host country.

[19]The World Bank, Somalia–World Development Indicators webpage, The World Bank, http://data.worldbank.org/country/somalia (accessed 1 March 2014).

[20]The Freedom House, Somalia, http://www.freedomhouse.org/country/somalia#.U27q7PldUXs (accessed 10 February 2014).

[21]RAND defines empire as: organizations that "seek to overthrow more than one regime and establish a single, sovereign authority, such as a caliphate." Al Shabaab has committed itself to conducting terrorist activities outside of the borders of Somalia and is interested in restoring ethnically Somali regions (such as the Ogaden) under its brand of sharia law.

[22]Note: The methodology of the RAND study does little to address the transnational nature of Al Qai'da compared to other terrorist organizations. The RAND study instead orients on the country in which terrorist organizations are founded or currently based in. In the case of Al Qai'da, this only has limited meaning and detracts from the overall purity of the study at it has been based in multiple countries simultaneously over the last few decades. That said, no social science analysis method is perfect and despite this shortcoming, we should not loose site of the overall value of the RAND study. With respect to the purity of the analysis, unlike Al Qaeda, Al Shabaab is geographically bound to one country, or rather one region (as described in Chapter 1).

violent practices and join the political process (43 percent). Otherwise, a terrorist group usually ends due to successful policing (40 percent). By comparison, military force is seldom successful and only accounts for only seven percent. The final way that terrorist groups end is due to achieving their objectives. Terrorist groups, on average, achieve their aims 10 percent of the time. Therefore, it appears that terrorist groups are more likely to win than they are to be destroyed by military force.[23] RAND also found that "terrorists fighting for broad goals, such as social revolution or empire, are less likely to reach a negotiated settlement than are groups fighting for limited aims, such as policy change or territorial change."[24] These are sobering statistics especially in light of the U.S. policies for confronting terrorism by military means over the last decade or so.

Figure 3.   How Terrorist Groups END (N = 268)

Source: Created by author utilizing data from Seth G. Jones and Martin C. Libicki; *How Terrorist Groups End: Lessons for Countering Al Qa'ida* (Santa Monica, CA: RAND Corporation, 2008), 45.

---

[23]Jones and Libicki, *How Terrorist Groups End*, 43-44.

[24]Ibid., 2.

Of the 648 terrorist groups considered (649 with the addition of Al Shabaab), 62 percent have ended and 34 percent remain active. However, the study also found that religiously affiliated terrorist groups are substantially less likely to end than non-religious terrorist groups. Of the religious terrorist groups, only 32 percent have ended and 68 percent remain active. Specifically, for the RAND study 45 individual religious terrorist groups ended, 26 splintered (and are still active as one or more terrorist organizations),[25] 13 fell to policing, three succumbed to military force, three of the groups abandoned terrorism to take on a political role, and none of the religious terrorist groups achieved their goals.[26]

Figure 4.   Profile of Religious Terrorist Groups

Source: Created by author utilizing data from Seth G. Jones and Martin C. Libicki; *How Terrorist Groups End: Lessons for Countering Al Qa'ida* (Santa Monica, CA: RAND Corporation, 2008), 36.

---

[25]The RAND study clearly counts splintered organizations as 'ended' organizations. This approach is a likely a flaw in the RAND methodology. By example, if a terrorist organization splits up and reemerges as two or more organizations with new names, but still committed to conducting acts of terrorism, then what has actually ended?

[26]Seth G. Jones and Martin C. Libicki, *How Terrorist Groups End: Lessons for Countering Al Qa'ida* (Santa Monica, RAND Corporation, 2009), 36.

With respect to Al Shabaab, the implications are arresting. The statistics indicate that Al Shabaab is unlikely to be eradicated. For comparison's sake, the RAND study found that Al Qai'da was also unlikely to end. The key difference between the two organizations (with respect to this line of quantitative analysis) is that Al Shabaab has greater membership. This is bad news as the bigger the terrorist organization; the less likely it is that it will end.[27] If Al Shabaab membership numbers continue to grow, then the problem is even more severe as terrorist organizations exceeding 10,000 members are among the most resilient. However, although religious terrorist groups are difficult to end, they are also unlikely to achieve their desired ends. Within the RAND study, no religious terrorist groups were able to fully achieve their desired end state.

Counterinsurgents in Somalia

With respect to counterinsurgent strength, the U.S. primarily uses an indirect approach in Somalia. Rather than directly sending its own military personnel, the U.S. has organized a military coalition through the African Union to help tackle the problems in Somalia. The African Union Mission in Somalia (AMISOM) was fielded in 2007 and has continued to grow in strength since that time. The U.S. has steadfastly provided material, logistics, and other support to AMISOM.[28]

---

[27]Jones and Libicki, *How Terrorist Groups End*, 64.

[28]Jen Psaki, " U.S. Welcomes Joint AMISOM-Somali National Army Efforts Against al-Shabaab," U.S. State Department, 12 March 2014, http://www.state.gov/r/pa/prs/ps/2014/03/223388.htm (accessed 27 May 2014); U.S. Mission to the African Union, "United States Mission to the African Union AMISOM/Somalia Fact Sheet," http://www.usau.usmission.gov/fact_sheet.html (accessed 27 May 2014).

This portion of research focuses on the Troop-to-Task ratios in Somalia and compares actual overall available counterinsurgent forces through the metrics recommend in U.S. Army Field Manual 3-24: Counterinsurgency (FM 3-24). Total counterinsurgent forces include available host nation police and military forces as well as guest forces. In the case of Somalia, this equation includes the combined strength of AMISOM. FM 3-24 recommends a total counterinsurgency strength of between 20 and 25 personnel to every 1,000 people within a given Area of Operations.[29] The FM offers the following caveat: "As in any conflict, the size of the force needed to defeat an insurgency depends on the situation. However, COIN is manpower intensive because counterinsurgents must maintain widespread order and security. Moreover, counterinsurgents typically have to adopt different approaches to address each element of the insurgency."[30] The caveat effectively means that the authors feel that the ratio of 20-25 to every 1000 residents may be insufficient in some situations. The suggested metric in FM 3-24 represent a new direction for the army with respect to counterinsurgency manpower. Previous U.S. Army doctrine for counterinsurgency ascribed manpower based on the geographic size of the area of operations rather than focusing on the size of the population within the area of operations. Table 6 provides the results of total available counterinsurgent strength over the last nine years.

---

[29]U.S. Army, Field Manual 3-24, *Counterinsurgency* (Washington, DC: Headquarters Department of the Army, December 2006), 1-67.

[30]Ibid., 1-68.

Table 6.   Available Counterinsurgent Strength in Somalia 2007–2014

Source: Created by author utilizing data from the AMISOM website, the United Nations Development Program (UNDP), and the Government of Somalia Police website.

Table 7 compares the population growth of Somalia against the ratios of troop strength recommend in FM 3-24. Research reveals that Somalia's population is growing at a fast pace. Along with much of Sub-Saharan Africa, Somalia's population is among the fastest growing in the world. The method of counterinsurgency spelled out in FM 3-24 recommends a ratio of troops compared to overall civilian population size. With this in mind the overall size of counterinsurgents must increase with the population.

Table 7.   Population and Recommended Counterinsurgent Strength (per FM 3-24)

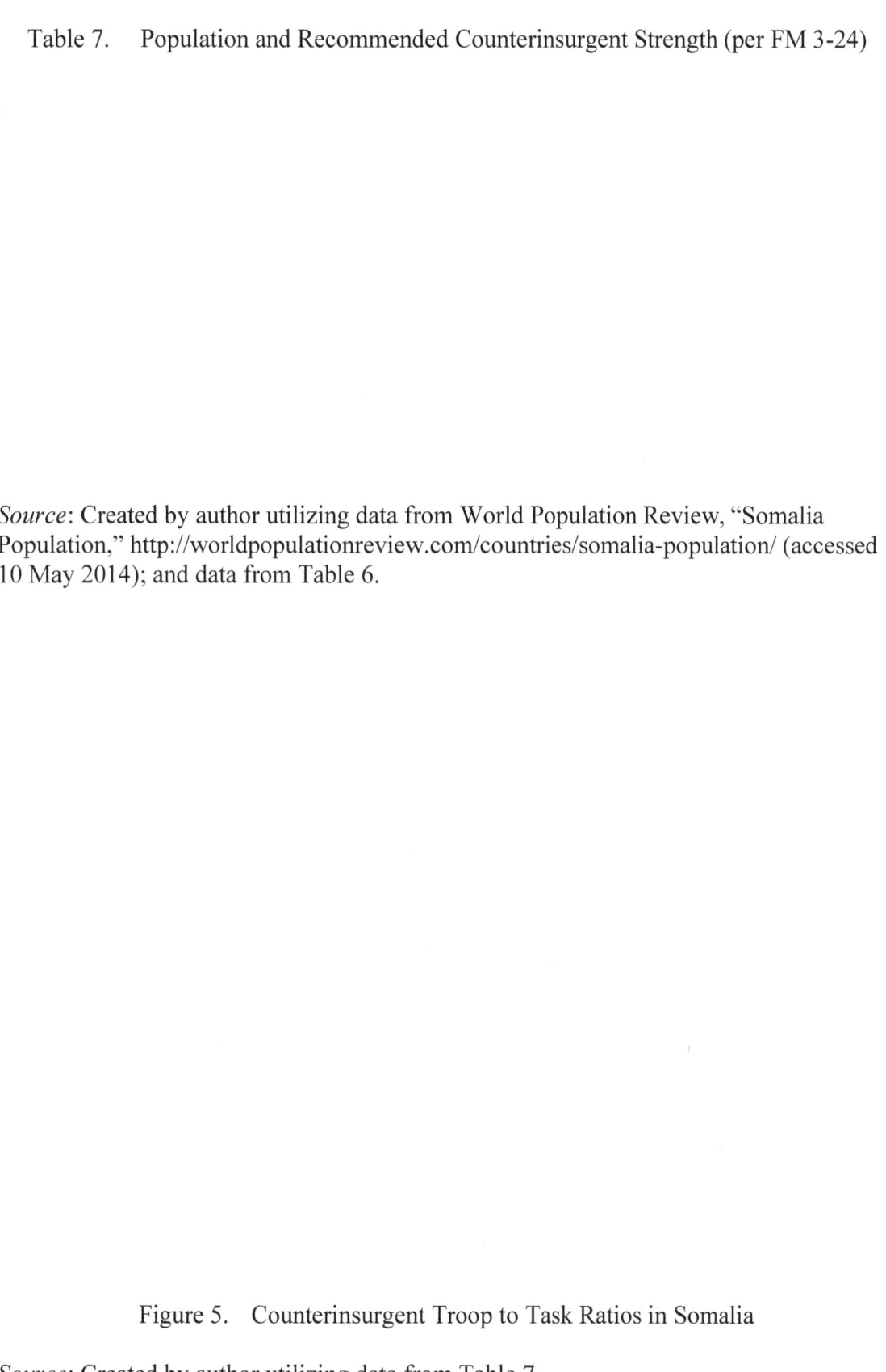

Source: Created by author utilizing data from World Population Review, "Somalia Population," http://worldpopulationreview.com/countries/somalia-population/ (accessed 10 May 2014); and data from Table 6.

Figure 5.   Counterinsurgent Troop to Task Ratios in Somalia

Source: Created by author utilizing data from Table 7.

The clear disconnect between actual counterinsurgent strength and the ratio that is recommend in the U.S. FM on counterinsurgency is alarming. Unfortunately, breaking the situation down to a closer view is no less alarming. Looking at police alone, Somalia has an overall police to population ratio of 1.7 police officers for every 1,000 inhabitants.[31]

Though some successes have been reported in the struggle against Al Shabaab, it appears that Somalia's security forces are indeed stretched thin. Recent reporting from both Western and African sources support this assertion. Private security and regional warlords, which do not cooperate with AMISOM, are more the norm.[32] Making the situation even worse, there is recent evidence of Somali police fighting Somali military personnel; a highly unproductive situation if true.[33] The following is an excerpt from an

---

[31]Note: By comparison the U.S., which is not dealing with a domestic insurgency, has 2.7 officers for every 1,000 residents in non-city areas. In its cities, the U.S. has an average ratio of 3.5 officers per every 1,000 residents. These statistics, which have been complied by the U.S. Federal Bureau of Investigation, include ratios for county and city police departments only. If State and Federal policing agencies are included, the ratios would be much higher. With these statistics, it is also important to keep in mind that the numbers are only averages, if individual U.S. cities are selected the ratios can become substantially larger. For example, Washington D.C. has 6.6 officers for every 1,000 residents; Federal Bureau of Investigation, "Police Employee Data" website, www2.fbi.gov/ucr/cius2009/police/, (accessed 1 May 2014); Governing.com, "Law Enforcement Officers Per Capita for Cities, Local Departments" webpage, www.governing.com/gov-data/safety-justice/law-enforcement-police-department-employee-totals-for-cities.html, (accessed on 1 May 2014).

[32]Mohamed Barack, "Mogadishu security declines as armed forces stretched outside capital," African Arguments, http://africanarguments.org/2014/04/16/mogadishu-security-declines-as-armed-forces-stretched-outside-capital-by-mohamed-mubarak/ (accessed 30 April 2014).

[33]AllAfrica.com, "Somalia - Military in Deadly Battle With Police in Middle Shabelle," http://allafrica.com/stories/201404181389.html (accessed 1 May 2014).

interview between Hamdi Salad (a reporter for Sabahi) and the Somali Minister of

Defense Mohamed Sheikh Hassan Hamud.

> *Sabahi*: "How many soldiers comprise the SNA and what are you doing to train them?"

> *Hamud*: "Starting in 2005, when the transitional government was formed, until now, there have been various efforts to provide training to soldiers under different [agreements] and in different countries. Nonetheless, it has been hard for [the government] to keep track of the army because when soldiers are done with training they are sent out to fight. Also, there are no standard military bases for the army. There are no renovated military bases even in the battlegrounds, and that has resulted in [an inability] to clearly define the true number of the army."[34]

Mr. Hamud's comments support the trend of confusion regarding the actual

number of Somali security forces currently available for duty. Better information exists

for how many soldiers have been trained as well as how many are on payroll. However,

widespread corruption has prevented these numbers from translating into actual available

troop strength. In some instances insubordination and dereliction has caused the dismissal

of hundreds of trained security personnel in recent months.[35]

Taken as a whole, analysis of the indirect approach (using AMISOM to further

U.S. interests) reveals a few big problems. While AMISOM is well manned with regards

to a conventional fight, it is significantly undermanned with regards to fighting an

insurgency (at least in terms of U.S. doctrine). AMISOM has achieved territorial gains

across southern and central Somalia. With respect to a conventional foe, territorial gains

---

[34]Hamdi Salad, "Somali Minister of Defence: Government committed to re-building army," *Sabahi* online, 25 March 2014, http://sabahionline.com/en_GB/articles/hoa/articles/features/2014/03/25/feature-01 (accessed 15 April 2014).

[35]Sabahi, "700 Somali soldiers fired for incompetence," *Sabahi*, 5 February 2014, http://sabahionline.com/en_GB/articles/hoa/articles/newsbriefs/2014/02/05/newsbrief-04 (accessed 15 March 2014).

would certainly serve as a strong measure of effectiveness. However, these gains do not equate to success against Al Shabaab which has clearly organized itself as an asymmetric insurgency and not as a conventional fighting force.

Afghanistan Case Study

This case study considers five elements and consequences (represented as categories) of U.S. policy for Afghanistan from 1981 to 2001 and draws a qualitative comparison with U.S. policy for Somalia from 1978 to 1993. The categories considered are engagement through proxy conflict, indirect funding of the proxy war, rapid withdraw of funding and support following success, and subsequent growth of a Muslim fundamentalist movement. While this portion of research includes discussion of some indirect methods, it ultimately orients on a direct approach on the part of the U.S. to eliminate a Muslim fundamentalist organization.

The U.S. proxy conflict with the Soviet Union in Afghanistan through the use of Pakistan's Inter Service Intelligence (ISI) and the Afghan Mujahedeen is both well studied and heavily reported on. In particular, the book: *Ghost Wars: The Secret History of the CIA, Afghanistan, and Bin Laden, from the Soviet Invasion to September 10, 2001* by Steve Coll, provides an excellent summary of the modern Great Game in Afghanistan leading up to the 11 September 2001 attacks.[36] Additionally, *Charlie Wilson's War* by George Crile is an excellent resource regarding the U.S. proxy war in Afghanistan during

---

[36]Steve Coll, *Ghost Wars: The Secret History of the CIA, Afghanistan, and Bin Laden, from the Soviet Invasion to September 10, 2001* (New York: Penguin Press, 2004).

the Soviet occupation.[37] During the conflict in Afghanistan; the Mujahedeen effort against the Soviets was funded indirectly by the U.S. through Pakistan's ISI; the ISI specifically focused on recruiting and advancing Muslim fundamentalist at the tactical level; U.S. funding was withdrawn from Afghan-related efforts following the war's success; and this resulted in a subsequent emergence of Muslim fundamentalist as the dominant element in Afghanistan. The ultimate outcome, as least prior to the 11 September 2001 terrorist attacks, is that the Taliban emerged as the principal power in Afghanistan.

Table 8.   Taliban Organizational Profile

Source: Created by author using data from Seth G. Jones and Martin C. Libicki; *How Terrorist Groups End: Lessons for Countering Al Qa'ida* (Santa Monica, CA: RAND Corporation, 2008), 181.

Like Al Shabaab, the Taliban is principally based in a country where the average annual income of an individual is low. As with Somalia, Afghanistan's Gross National Income is in the bottom percentage of all nations (Category: L).[38] The Freedom House

---

[37]George Crile, *Charlie Wilson's War* (New York: Grove Press, 2003).

[38]The World Bank, Somalia – World Development Indicators webpage, http://data.worldbank.org/country/Afghanistan, (accessed 15 May 2014).

rankings for freedom of the press appoint Afghanistan in the second lowest rating bracket of Not Free (Category: PF).[39] However, prior to the North Atlantic Treaty Organization (NATO) mission to Afghanistan, Afghanistan fell in the lowest freedom of the press rating bracket. If the U.S. fully withdraws from Afghanistan that it is possible that the country will again be in the bottom bracket. The Taliban is an organization driven principally by religious beliefs (Category: R). Finally, the Taliban is committed to the goal of establishing regime change (Category: RC). Like Al Shabaab, the Taliban has not ended (Category: *Null*).

Somalia's Cold War period has received far less literary attention than Afghanistan, especially in the last ten years. However, sufficient information exists to trace a meaningful comparison between the two conflicts.

In the mid-1970s, the Soviet Union was well engaged with Siad Barre's Somalia and provided both economic and military aid. However, following the 12 September 1974 coup by the Marxist Derg against Ethiopia's monarchy, the Soviet Union expanded its Horn of Africa focus to Ethiopia. The civil war in Ethiopia greatly weakened the military might of the nation. Consequently, Somalia's ruler Siad Barre saw an opportunity to restore the Ogaden (a historical and ethnically Somali region of Ethiopia) to Somalia. Some sources assert that, as part of this effort, Barre transitioned away from the Soviets and began to court the U.S. and pro-western entities to support his regime.[40]

---

[39]The Freedom House, "Somalia," http://www.freedomhouse.org/country/somalia#.U27q7PldUXs (accessed 10 February 2014).

[40]Executive Intelligence Review, "Somalia Breaks with Soviet Union, Cuba: The Somalia Story: A Year of Diplomatic Warfare," *Executive Intelligence Review* 4, no.47 (November 1977): 54.

Others have asserted that despite the eventual transition, Barre tried to maintain positive relations with the Soviet Union for as long as possible. In either case, it seems clear that eventually Barre oriented himself firmly in the direction of Washington. This western stance on the part of Somalia did not appear overt until sometime after the conclusion of the 1977-1978 Ogaden War. Despite some sources indicating a different view, it is important to note that the Ogaden War of 13 July 1977 to 15 March 1978 is generally not viewed as a proxy war between the U.S. and the Soviet Union.[41] However, the period following the 1977-1978 Ogaden War can be viewed, increasingly over time, as a proxy conflict between the U.S. and the Soviets. The proxy conflict was cemented by the 1982 Ethiopian-Somali Border War which took place primarily on the Somali side of the Ogaden.[42] The Soviets continued to back the Ethiopians during this period. Consequently, in keeping with the 1950 National Security Council Report 68 (NSC 68) policy directive, the U.S. backed the Somalis with arms and other aid as part of a broader worldwide policy of containment.

The U.S. penchant for entering limited conflicts during the Cold War was driven by NSC 68, which served as the foundational document to the U.S. strategy of

---

[41]Note: Some evidence suggests that the U.S. may have been covertly supporting Somalia as early as 1977: Odd Arne Westad, *The Global Cold War* (Cambridge University Press, 2005), 261 "(President) Carter's message was clear: the United States would not get directly involved in the ongoing war, but was willing to support Somalia covertly and by proxy."

[42]Alan Cowell, "Guerrilla Drive in Somalia seen as part of a Proxy War," *The New York Times*, 16 July 1982, http://www.nytimes.com/1982/07/16/world/guerrilla-drive-in-somalia-seens-as-part-of-a-proxy-war.html, (accessed 18 April 2014).

containment against the Soviets.[43] In keeping with NSC 68 strategy, the U.S. sought to avoid direct military confrontation with the Soviet Union but also sought to block the expansion of Soviet ideology geographically through indirect means. In other words, where the Soviets went the U.S. would seek to prevent their progress, but not by direct means. That the Soviets backed Ethiopia and that Ethiopia was fighting the Somalis, made backing Somalia a priority for the U.S. in terms of the NSC 68 policy. NSC 68 was developed from a classified whitepaper (the "Long Telegram") by George Kennan, who was the Deputy Chief of Mission at the U.S. embassy in Moscow in the late 1940s.[44] Kennan's paper was published anonymously by "X" in 1947 with the title of "The Sources of Soviet Conduct."[45] In the article, Kennan advocates for a softer and more patient approach than was ultimately implemented under NSC 68. Many policy makers tended to view both the Cold War as well as the U.S. policy spelled out in NSC 68 as a zero sum game.[46] However, not all senior policy makers viewed NSC 68 in the same black and white perspective. Henery Kissinger, former U.S. Secretary of State and National Security Advisor, wrote that:

> For all of its ostensibly hardheaded realism, NSC-68 began with a peroration on democracy and concluded with the assertion that history would ultimately work in

---

[43]Office of the Historian, "NSC 68, 1950," U.S. Department of State, http://history.state.gov/milestones/1945-1952/NSC68 (accessed 15 February 2014).

[44]Office of the Historian, "Kennan and Containment," U.S. Department of State, http://history.state.gov/milestones/1945-1952/kennan (accessed 19 May 2014).

[45]George F. Kennan, "The Sources of Soviet Conduct," *Foreign Policy*, July 1947, http://www.foreignaffairs.com/articles/23331/x/the-sources-of-soviet-conduct (accessed 20 May 2014).

[46]David Ryan, *US Foreign Policy in World History; The New International History* (New York: Routledge, 2014), 138.

America's favor. What was unique about this document was its coupling of universal claims with the renunciation of force. Never before had a Great Power expressed objectives quite so demanding of its own resources without any expectation of reciprocity other than the dissemination of its national values. And these would be achieved thorough global reform, not global conquest, the usual path of crusaders.[47]

In essence, Kissinger, like some other former senior U.S. policy makers, held a more dynamic view of NSC 68 and avoided viewing U.S. policy exclusively from a hardheaded realist point of view.

In addition to the increase in U.S. funding the Somali's enjoyed substantial support from U.S. partners. By example, Saudi Arabia pledged $300 million dollars in support of Somalia's effort against the Ethiopians (Soviets).[48]

The majority of the Somali combatants in the Ogaden War, and the subsequent border fighting in the 1980s and early 1990s, were conservative Muslims.[49] However, it is important to note that the cause of the fighting appears not to have been driven by religion. The conflict was instead driven initially by territorial aspirations (Barre's desire to restore the Ogaden to Somalia). As with Afghanistan, while the leaders may have had geopolitical reasons at the strategic level, religion played a major role in the conflict at the tactical level.[50]

---

[47]Hennery Kissinger, *Diplomacy* (New York: Simon and Schuster, 1994), 463.

[48]Kenneth Weiss, "The Soviet Involvement in The Ogaden War" (Professional Paper, Center for Naval Analyses, 1980), 10.

[49]Alex de Waal, *Islamism and Its Enemies in the Horn of Africa* (Bloomington: Indiana University Press, 2004), 9.

[50]Mohammed Mealin Seid, "The Role of Religion In The Ogaden Conflict," Social Science Research Council, 26 January 2009, http://hornofafrica.ssrc.org/ mealin/printable.html; (accessed 15 April 2014).

Barre endured a tapering of U.S. funding as the Ethiopian-Somali proxy conflict

cooled down in the late 1980s.[51] It may be possible to argue that the funding dwindled as

a result of the Cold War as a whole drawing to a close during the same period. Table 8

provides historical U.S. financial support for Somalia over the last two and a half decades

and includes Department of State, Department of Defense, and USAID funding.

Figure 6.   U.S. Financial Support to Somalia

Source: Created by author utilizing data from USAID, CRS Reports for Congress, and
the World Bank. Note: Numbers presented for fiscal year 2014 are tentative due to
publication date of this document. Final fiscal year 2014 numbers will not be available
until after the year-end close out.

---

[51]Gregory A. Pirio, *The African Jihad: Bin Laden's quest for the horn of Africa*
(Trenton: The Red Sea Press, 2007), 45.

It is important to note that the information presented in Table 8 is not representative of the full extent of the U.S. economic instrument of national power. For instance, the U.S. frequently utilizes the International Monetary Fund (IMF), which are not included in table 8, as a vehicle to support developing countries.[52] Additionally, depending on the circumstances, different parties within the international community sometimes collaboratively take the lead in supporting specific developing countries. In the case of Somalia, both the United Kingdom and Italy have been major donors over the last two decades.[53]

Table 10, which was created by Global Humanitarian Assistance, summarizes overall international humanitarian assistance to Somalia between 1990 and 2010. The report does not include military assistance or other non-humanitarian spending. Though covering a slightly different period, the trends revealed in Table 9 and Table 10 are similar in many respects. Table 10 shows a big dip at the end of the Barre period (1991), followed by a massive increase coinciding with the UNITAF, UNISOM, and Operation

---

[52]Note: the IMF has been inactive for the last 22 years in Somalia. However, the IMF was an important aspect of the Barre regime's financial health; IMF, "IMF Recognizes the Federal Government of Somalia After 22-year Interval," IMF, 12 April 2013, https://www.imf.org/external/np/sec/pr/2013/pr13119.htm (accessed 22 May 2014); IMF, "IMF Recognizes the Federal Government of Somalia After 22-year Interval," IMF, 12 April 2013, https://www.imf.org/external/np/sec/pr/2013/pr13119.htm (accessed 22 May 2014).

[53]Note: At different periods in history, large portions of Somalia fell under both Italian and British colonial rule respectively; Tom Kelly and Tim Shipman, "Foreign aid to Somalia 'helps Al Qaeda': Pressure grows to divert cash back to the UK," *Mail online*, 23 February 2014, http://www.dailymail.co.uk/news/article-2566310/90m-British-aid-Somalia-helps-Al-Qaeda-Pressure-grows-divert-cash-UK.html (accessed 12 May 2014); Farnesina, "Somalia: Italy's role for regional stability," *Farnesina*, 25 August 2010, http://www.esteri.it/MAE/EN/Sala_Stampa/ArchivioNotizie/Approfondimenti/2010/08/20100825_Somalia.htm (accessed 20 May 2014).

Provide Relief missions. Funding then drops significantly before slowly building up again. Global Humanitarian Assistance summarizes the funding changes in the following way:

> Official development assistance (ODA) to Somalia fell sharply in the period after United States (US) military and United Nations (UN) peacekeeping troops withdrew in 1994 and 1995, and only began to increase substantially in the period around the US-backed Ethiopian invasion in 2006. (Official Development Assistance) doubled between 2007 and 2008 as insecurity and declining access to food drove a major deterioration in the humanitarian situation.[54]

Figure 7.   International Humanitarian Assistance to Somalia

Source: Global Humanitarian Assistance, "International financing investments," 21 February 2012, http://www.globalhumanitarianassistance.org/wp-content/uploads/ 2012/02/gha-somalia-briefing-paper-feb-2012-final.pdf (accessed 20 April 2014), 3.

---

[54]Global Humanitarian Assistance, "International financing investments" 21 February 2012, http://www.globalhumanitarianassistance.org/wp-content/uploads/2012/ 02/gha-somalia-briefing-paper-feb-2012-final.pdf (accessed 20 April 2014), 3.

Following the conclusion of the Cold War, Barre's regime in Somalia survived until 1992 before ultimately falling apart. The following year, famine struck Somalia and the country descended into what many have described as complete chaos.[55] The fall of the Barre regime coupled with famine, the emergence of warlords, and chaos brought about a robust international response in the form of the UNITAF, UNISOM, and Operation Provide Relief missions. These missions also came with a host of associated international attention and funding.[56] However the political fallout of the so called 'Blackhawk Down event' and its partner, the 'CNN effect,' brought these missions to an unsuccessful and early conclusion.[57]

Somalia remained in an overall state of lawlessness for the next several years. However, nestled within the chaos, some individual clans and warlords began to stand up sharia courts in order to bring a sense of stability to their respective territory. The first court was established in northern Mogadishu by one of the Hawiye's sub-clans in 1994.[58] The court was perceived as an improvement from the lawlessness that previously prevailed and the system was adopted in neighboring clans and sub-clans in and around Mogadishu through the mid and late 1990s. In April of 1999 some of the courts organized

---

[55]Jane Perlez, "Bush Sees Victims of Somali Famine," *The New York Times*, 1 January 1993, http://www.nytimes.com/1993/01/01/world/bush-sees-victims-of-somali-famine.html (accessed 10 May 2014).

[56]The large spike in table 9 is the result of U.S. financial and material support for the UNITAF, UNISOM, UNISOM II and Operation Provide Relief missions in Somalia.

[57]Robert G. Patman, *Strategic Shortfall: The Somalia Syndrome and the March to 9/11* (Santa Barbara: ABC-CLIO, 2010), 41-65.

[58]Cedric Barnes and Harun Hassan, *The Rise and Fall of Mogadishu's Islamic Courts* (London: Chatham House, 2007), 2.

into the Joint Islamic Council (JIC). However, the JIC soon fell apart as it was comprised from only one clan and lacked broad support.[59] During the next four years, several individual Islamic courts and Islamic court coalitions formed and disintegrated in and around southern and central Somalia with an overall trend of declining influence. The down trend in the individual and small unions of Islamic courts during this time has been attributed, at least in part, to edicts of the Somali Transitional Federal Government (TFG).[60] Unfortunately, the TFG was not able or ready to provide a viable alternative to the judicial system of the Islamic courts in south and central Somalia. Finally in late 2003, a school teacher by the name of Sheikh Sharif Sheikh Ahmed revived the Islamic courts in northern Mogadishu out of concern over the ongoing lawlessness. Ahmed's effort was perceived as a success locally and additional courts were established throughout the Mogadishu region. In late 2004 Ahmed was elected as Chairman of all Islamic Courts in the region.[61] This organization soon assumed the name Islamic Courts Union (ICU). The relative success of the ICU created tension with regional warlords in Mogadishu and across southern and central Somalia. This tension in turn led to additional violence between the various factions which undermined the effectiveness of the ICU's judicial system.

An additional factor to the developing conflict in southern Somalia was the influx of former members of *Al-Itihaad Al-Islaam* ('The Islamic Union'–also known as *Al*

---

[59]Stig Jarle Hansen, *Al-Shabaab in Somalia: The History and Ideology of a Militant Islamist Group* (London: C. Hurst and Company, 2013), 34.

[60]Cedric Barnes and Harun Hassan, *The Rise and Fall of Mogadishu's Islamic Courts* (London: Chatham House, 2007), 3.

[61]Ibid., 2.

Itihaad or AIAI) into the Mogadishu area. Al Itihaad was a prominent political and paramilitary organization during the early 1990s and fought against the various warlords of the era. Al Itihaad was stanchly Wahhabist in its ideology and had direct ties to Al Qaeda as well as Osama Bin Laden while he resided in the Sudan.[62] Aggravated by multiple attacks within its territory, the Ethiopian military took steps to dismantle Al Itihaad which was based in the city of Gedo in the mid-1990s. By the end of 1996 Al Itihaad was considered to be militarily defunct and many of its former members fled to the Mogadishu area. Former Al Itihaad leaders, like Sheikh Aweys who had previously partnered with Al Qaeda, eventually joined the ICU and began to assert their Wahhabist ideology into the organization.[63] By the middle of 2006 Aweys became the leader of the *Mujlis al-Shura* (Consultative Council), which was the policy making body of the ICU. This was an ill omen for opponents of radical Islam in Somalia.

> With Sheikh Aweys at the helm of the Islamic Courts, it was as if the worse-case counterterrorism scenario was unfolding. For years, counterterrorism analyst had been warning that stateless Somalia had the potential of becoming a haven for Al Qaeda and other international jihadist groups just as what had occurred in Afghanistan under the rule of the Taliban.[64]

In 2005, Mogadishu was subject to several unexplained disappearances and killings of top level leaders of specific clans and courts.[65] The prevailing perception is that some of the regional warlords had partnered with covert U.S. entities to eliminate or

---

[62]Pirio, *The African Jihad,* 46.

[63]Eliza Griswold, *The Tenth Parallel: Dispatches from the Fault Line between Christianity and Islam* (New York: Macmillan, 2010), 147; Pirio, *The African Jihad*, 2.

[64]Pirio, *The African Jihad,* 3.

[65]Cedric Barnes and Harun Hassan, *The Rise and Fall of Mogadishu's Islamic Courts* (London: Chatham House, 2007), 3.

at least greatly undermine the ICU.[66] Other sources have asserted that it was the TFG rather than regional warlords who facilitated the targeting of ICU leaders with the support of U.S. covert operators.[67] Due to the severity of the threat, new militias formed in and around Mogadishu under the auspices of providing protection for the ICU. One of the militias assumed the name *Al Shabaab* (the Youth). While Al Shabaab was formed out of a perceived need to support and protect the ICU, it would not be accurate to say that they were the same organization. Nor would it be accurate to say that the ICU exercised any real supervisory authority over the militias. Al Shabaab was "related to but seemingly autonomous of the broad-based Courts movement."[68] In the first half of 2006 the ICU with the aid of Al Shabaab and other affiliated militias pushed the warlords out of Mogadishu. At which time "the Courts (ICU) achieved the unthinkable, uniting Mogadishu for the first time in 16 years, and re-established peace and security."[69]

---

[66]Chris Talbot, "US Continues Covert Action In Somalia," *The Somaliland Times*, 27 September 2006, http://somalilandtimes.net/sl/2005/245/11.shtml (accessed 22 May 2014), para 3; Michael Kelly, "US Special Ops Have Become Much, Much Scarier Since 9/11," *Business Insider,* 10 May 2013, http://www.businessinsider.com/the-rise-of-jsoc-in-dirty-wars-2013-4 (accessed 20 May 2014), para 11; Linda J. Bilmes and Michael D. Intriligator, "How Many Wars Is the US Fighting Today?" *Peace Economic, Peace Science, and Public Policy* 19, no. 1 (2013): 10.

[67]Jeremy Scahill, "The CIA's Secret Sites in Somalia," *The Nation*, 12 July 2012, http://www.thenation.com/article/161936/cias-secret-sites-somalia (accessed 20 May 2014), para 9; Sean D. Naylor, "The Secret War: Africa Ops May Be Just Starting," *The Army Times*, 5 December 2011, http://www.armytimes.com/article/20111205/NEWS/112050312/The-Secret-War-Africa-ops-may-just-starting (accessed 22 May 2014); Drones Team, "Somalia: reported US covert actions 2001-2014," *The Bureau of Investigative Journalism,* 22 February 2012, http://www.thebureauinvestigates.com/2012/02/22/get-the-data-somalias-hidden-war/ (accessed 22 May 2014).

[68]Barnes and Hassan, *The Rise and Fall of Mogadishu's Islamic Courts*, 3.

[69]Ibid., 4.

As touched on earlier in this chapter, while the ICU was in the process of further consolidating its power in southern and central Somalia, U.S. backed Ethiopian troops removed them from power in latter half of 2006 and early 2007. This move was at first hailed as a success from the western point of view.[70] However, over time the deliberate destruction of the ICU has come to be seen as a blunder. The NGO Global Humanitarian Assistance described the transition in the following way:

> Somalia's humanitarian crisis has increased in scale and severity since 2007, following the US-backed Ethiopian-led military invasion in support of the TFG, which ousted the radical Islamist Union of Islamic Courts. After Ethiopian troops withdrew in 2009, and despite the presence of an African Union peacekeeping force, the al-Qaeda-linked Islamist group al-Shabab regained control of large parts of the country.
>
> Worsening insecurity after the 2007 invasion precipitated a dramatic deterioration in the humanitarian situation resulting in large-scale displacements. Attacks on aid workers sharply increased further diminishing already restricted humanitarian access to vulnerable populations.[71]

The British news giant *The Guardian* has also been retrospectively unsympathetic to the U.S. approach:

> what should have been a Somali problem, requiring a Somali solution to address militancy within the ICU, became an Ethiopian and American problem. The end result was more anarchy in Somalia that now had no chance at a central authority, and the birth of al-Shabab.

---

[70]Steve Schippert, "al-Qaeda and the ICU's Somali Retreat," Threats Watch, 2 January 2007, http://threatswatch.org/inbrief/2007/01/alqaeda-and-the-icus-somali-re/ (accessed on 19 May 2014).

[71]Global Humanitarian Assistance, "International financing investments," 21 February 2012, http://www.globalhumanitarianassistance.org/wp-content/uploads/2012/02/gha-somalia-briefing-paper-feb-2012-final.pdf (accessed 20 April 2014), 4.

In the long run, the ICU might have united Somalia into a country that had the interests of the majority at its heart–or one that was to become an outpost of terror. The point is that we don't know.[72]

The common thread from all sources is that the U.S. perceived the ICU to be a threat and facilitated its demise with a heavy handed and direct approach. Al Shabaab, which was always more militant in nature . . . rather than judicial, survived the Ethiopian led dismantlement of the ICU, and has subsequently asserted itself as an aggressive terrorist organization across ethnically Somali regions. Western sources also consistently agree that Al Shabaab is decidedly worse than the ICU with respect to U.S. interests and regional stability. Destroying the ICU can be seen as scratching a poison ivy infection: the result of scratching poison ivy is a larger infection. Proper treatment of poison ivy requires patience and less aggressive solutions. With respect to U.S. policy, this means that nonmilitary methods may have yielded better results in the long run.

---

[72]Mukoma Wa Ngugi, "How al-Shabaab was born," The Guardian, 4 October 2013, http://www.theguardian.com/world/2013/oct/04/kenya-westgate-mall-attacks (accessed on 22 May 2014), para 4-5.

Table 9.   Afghanistan Case Study Results

Category	**Afghanistan**	**Somalia**
Proxy Conflict	Yes - U.S backed Mujahidin against Soviets in Afghanistan	Yes - U.S. backed Somalis against Soviet backed Ethiopians
Indirect funding motivated by policy of containment	Yes - Funding funneled through Pakistan ISI	No
Leveraging Muslim Fundamentalist	Yes - Islam leveraged at the tactical level	Yes - Islam leveraged at the tactical level
Pull back of U.S. funds following success against Soviets	Yes	Yes
Subsequent Growth of Muslim Fundamentalist movement	Yes - Taliban	Yes - Islamic Courts Union and Al Shabaab

Source: Created by author utilizing analysis from the case study.

Iran Case Study

This case study considers four elements and consequences (represented as categories) of U.S. policy for Iran from 1956 to the early 1980s and draws a qualitative comparison with U.S. policy for Somalia. The categories considered are discovery of natural resources, subsequent involvement of U.S. (or U.S. Allied) natural resource corporations, manipulation of host government, and emergence of Islamic fundamentalist organizations.

Unlike the previous case study on Afghanistan, this topic is less reported on and not well understood. Following the chaos of WWII Iran was an emerging democracy and in 1951, Mohammed Mossadegh became Prime Minister. At the outset, Mossadegh was quite popular and even earned honors as the Time Magazine Person of the Year in 1951. Thinking to capitalize on his success, he greatly increased his support of the domestic movement to nationalize Iran's oil reserves with the aim of controlling profits from the natural resource industry.[73] The British oil companies, then running natural resource production in Iran, did not take kindly to this notion. However, in 1953 Mossadegh followed through with his intentions and nationalized his country's oil reserves. This action proved to be a grave miscalculation. Within weeks the U.S. and the British initiated Operation AJAX which orchestrated the successful overthrow of Mohamed Mossadegh.[74] The U.S. then reinstalled Mohammad Reza Pahlavi as the Shah (monarch) who assisted with transition of control of Iran's natural resources back into Western hands. The new government was not popular, nor was it elected, and by the 1970s Iran became less stable. In 1978 major demonstrations were organized and before the end of the year the Shah was overthrown and a fundamentalist Islamic government emerged in Iran. The new government which exists to this day carries heavy anti-American sentiment and remains counter to U.S. interests in many of its actions. In particular, Iran's backing of the terrorist organization Hizballah (also known as Hezbollah, Hizbollah, and

---

[73]Mark j. Gasiorowski and Malcome Byrne, *Mohammad Mosaddeq and the 1953 Coup in Iran* (Syracuse, NY: Syracuse University Press, 2004), 261-277.

[74]Stephen Kinzer, *All the Shah's Men, An American Coup and the Roots of Middle East Terror* (New York: John Wiley and Sons, 2003).

Hizbu'llah among other names) has been particularly stinging to U.S. interests in the Levant.

Hizballah was founded in the aftermath of Israel's 1982 invasion of southern Lebanon which was conducted in order to remove pro-Palestinian militants operating in the area.[75] From its inception, Hizballah has considered itself to be an extension of the 1978 Iranian Revolution and is formally aligned as an adherent to the teachings and philosophy of Ayatollah Khomeini (founder of the Islamic Republic of Iran).[76] Hizballah made waves both early and often with attacks on the U.S. embassy in Beirut, the U.S. Marine Corps barracks in Beirut, the U.S. embassy annex in Beirut, Khobar Towers as well as several other well documented incidents.[77] Hizballah has grown in size, ambition, and prestige since its earliest days and is now widely considered to be a state within a state in southern Lebanon.[78] Table 11 describes the organizational profile for Hizballah as provided in the RAND study.

---

[75]Jonathan Masters and Zachary Laub, "Hezbollah," Council on Foreign Relations, 3 January 2014, http://www.cfr.org/lebanon/hezbollah-k-hizbollah-hizbullah/p9155 (accessed 22 May 2014), para 2.

[76]John Pike, Hizballah, "Party of God, Islamic Jihad, Islamic Jihad for the Liberation of Palestine, Organization of the Oppressed on Earth, Revolutionary Justice Organization," *Federation of American Scientists*, 18 March 2005, http://www.fas.org/irp/world/para/hizballah.htm (accessed 21 May 2014), para 3.

[77]The National Counterterrorism Center, "Hizballah," The National Counterterrorism Center, http://www.nctc.gov/site/groups/hizballah.html (accessed 22 May 2014).

[78]Josh Wood, "Hezbollah Rolls The Dice in Syria," Aljazeera America, 10 September 2013, http://america.aljazeera.com/articles/2013/9/10/hezbollah-rolls-thediceinsyria.html (accessed 20 May 2014), para 18; Samia Nakhoul, "Analysis: Hezbollah tips Syria power balance, polarizes Lebanon," http://www.reuters.com/article/2013/06/11/us-syria-hezbollah-conflict-analysis-idUSBRE95A0XS20130611 (accessed 21 May 2014), para 21.

Table 10.   Hizballah Organizational Profile

Source: Seth G. Jones and Martin C. Libicki; *How Terrorist Groups End: Lessons for Countering Al Qa'ida* (Santa Monica, CA: RAND Corporation, 2008), 160.

Unlike Al Shabaab, Hizballah is principally based in a country where the average annual income of an individual is in the upper middle of all countries (Category: UM).[79] The Freedom House rankings for freedom of the press appoint Lebanon in the second lowest category of Partially Free (Category: PF). Hizballah is an organization driven by religious beliefs prescribed by the late Ayatollah Khomeini (Category: R). According to RAND, Hizballah is committed to the goal of regime change (category: RC). However, given Hisballah's obvious willingness to conduct operations in multiple countries (Lebanon, Syria, Israel, and Iraq) paired with their goal of establishing widespread theocratic governance, it is difficult perceive why RAND did not consider the

[79]Note: Given Lebanon's problems and history of domestic strife it is difficult at first to believe that the country falls in the UM category. However, cross reference the World Bank webpage for Lebanon reveals that the RAND study is accurate in this category. Iran also fall in the UM category; The World Bank, "Lebanon," http://data.worldbank.org/country/Lebanon (accessed 20 May 2014); The World Bank, "Iran," http://data.worldbank.org/country/iran-islamic-republic (accessed 20 May 2014).

organization's aim as being empire (Category E).[80] Like Al Shabaab, Hizballah has not

ended (Category: Null).

On the surface, Somalia may appear to be nothing like Iran. However, Somalia is

in fact sitting on a sizable volume of natural resources. Several sources indicate that

multiple western natural resource companies (specifically: Conoco, Amoco, Chevron and

Phillips) have been eyeing Somalia's potential since at least 1991, and that these

companies made formal arrangements with the Barre regime shortly before its fall.[81]

Interest in the country's natural resources continues to this day and may prove to be a

source of conflict in the near future.[82] A portion of the impending problem revolves

around the establishment of international business agreements with the semi-autonomous

regions of Puntland and Somaliland as well as legacy agreements made by Barre's

---

[80]Note: RAND defines empire as: organizations that "seek to overthrow more than one regime and establish a single, sovereign authority, such as a caliphate." Jones and Libicki, *How Terrorist Groups End*, 18.

[81]U.N. Security Council; "Report of the Monitoring Group on Somalia and Eritrea pursuant to Security Council resolution 2060 (2012): Somalia," United Nations, 12 July 2013, 25; Mark Fineman, "The Oil Factor In Somalia," *Los Angeles Times*, 18 January 1993, http://articles.latimes.com/1993-01-18/news/mn-1337_1_oil-reserves (accessed 1 April 2014); Kalif, "America's interests in Somalia: Four major U.S. oil companies are sitting on a prospective fortune in exclusive concessions." Global Research, 3 January 2007, http://www.globalresearch.ca/america-s-interests-in-somalia-four-major-u-s-oil-companies-are-sitting-on-a-prospective-fortune-in-exclusive-concessions/4342 (accessed 20 April 2014); Sarah Young, "Somalia favours firms with pre-1991 deals for oil exploration," *Reuters*, 2 October 2012, http://www.reuters.com/article/2012/10/02/somalia-oil-exploration-idUSL6E8L2O7D20121002 (accessed 10 March 2014).

[82]Michelle Nichols and Louis Charbonneau, "Exclusive: Western oil exploration in Somalia may spark conflict – U.N. report," *Chicago Tribune*, 17 July 2013, http://www.reuters.com/article/2013/07/17/us-somalia-oil-un-idUSBRE96G0HZ 20130717 (accessed 12 March 2014).

successors in Mogadishu. The bottom line being that, with respect to this part of the analysis, western interest in Somalia's natural resource potential is mounting.

Manipulation of the host government seems not to be a factor in Somalia; at least not in the grand and dramatic way that occurred in Iran in 1953. While it may be true that the U.S. withdraw of funds contributed to Barre's downfall and the subsequent churn of civil war, there is no evidence that the U.S. wanted Barre to fail. However, evidence clearly suggests that the U.S. covertly undermined the Islamic Courts Union, which while not-pro U.S., was arguably a functional government with forward momentum.[83] That having been said, the ICU was not an internationally recognized body and cannot truly be considered in the same light as the removal of Mohamed Mossadegh. The internationally recognized government in Somalia during 2006, when the ICU was at its peak, was the Somalia TFG. This distinction is in some ways ironic as the ICU was actually 'governing,' while the TFG was only a nominal governmental body at that time.

The emergence of the ICU and the subsequent emergence of Al Shabaab has been discussed in detail in the previous case study.

---

[83]Emily Wax and Karen DeYoung, "U.S. Secretly Backing Warlords in Somalia," *Washington Post,* 17 May 2006, http://www.washingtonpost.com/wp-dyn/content/article/2006/05/16/AR2006051601625.html (accessed 11May 2014); Mark Mazzetti, "Efforts by CIA Fail in Somalia, Officials Charge," *The New York Times*, 8 June 2006, http://www.nytimes.com/2006/06/08/world/africa/08intel.html?pagewanted=all&_r=0 (accessed 10 April 2014).

Table 11. Iran Case Study Results

Category	Iran	Somalia
Discovery of Natural Resources	Yes	Yes
Subsequent Involvement of U.S. (or U.S. Allied) natural resource corporations	Yes - Western powers developed, fought over, and redeveloped Iran's natural resource industry	Yes - U.S. oil company involvement predates the fall of the Barre regime
Manipulation of host government	Yes - Operation AJAX	No - U.S. withdrawal of funding contributed to the Barre fall. However, it was not a U.S. policy that Barre fail.
Emergence of Islamic Fundamentalist organizations	Yes - Hizballah	Yes - Islamic Courts Union and Al Shabaab

Source: Created by author utilizing analysis from the case study.

CHAPTER 5

CONCLUSION

The primary research question asked: Are U.S. policies for Somalia effective? Analysis reveals that U.S. policies have been not been effective due to failure on the part of the U.S. to be committed and consistent in its policy approach over time and due to an inappropriate application of military force. As a result, the Al Shabaab terrorist organization has been created and has grown in strength and notoriety.

The U.S. backed African Union Mission in Somalia (AMISOM) continues to increase troop numbers and to achieve territorial gains. These geographically-based gains make sense in regards to a conventional foe. However, Al Shabaab has transitioned from a being a militia with conventional features into an asymmetric actor. Widely accepted troop-to-task ratios for counterinsurgency operations reveal that the total available counterinsurgent force (the combination of AMISOM plus Somalia's domestic police and military forces) present in Somalia appears to be significantly insufficient to accomplish the defeat of the Al Shabaab terrorist organization.

Analyzing statistics from 649 terrorist organizations reveals that Al Shabaab has a formidable organizational profile. By comparison with other terrorist organizations, it will be extremely difficult to end. However, as a religious terrorist organization with broad objectives it is not likely that Al Shabaab will be able to achieve its desired end state.

Research revealed that in some respects, U.S. policy for Somalia has resembled U.S. policies in Afghanistan during the Cold War. Like Afghanistan, Somalia was the scene of a proxy struggle, between the United States and the Soviet Union. And like that conflict, after achieving its aims, the U.S. backed away from providing support to the proxy nation. Additionally, U.S. policy for Somalia has at times resembled aspects of U.S. policy for Iran during the mid-twentieth century. In a parallel with Iran, Somalia may possess an important quantity of natural resources. Additionally, as with the mismanagement of U.S. policy for Iran during the mid-twentieth century, the inconsistent management of U.S. policy for Somalia may have led to the emergence of Al Shabaab. In the case of Iran the U.S. engineered the removal of a burgeoning democracy and installed a monarchy (Operation AJAX) in order to better secure access to Iranian natural resources. A few decades later, the Iranian revolution, which was in part a reaction to U.S. policies, led to the vehemently anti-U.S. and theocratic Islamic Republic of Iran which has been labeled as a state sponsor of terrorism by the U.S. due to its consistent support for Hizballah.

In Somalia, the pro-U.S. Barre regime fell apart following a severe tapering of both U.S and international funding in the closing years of the Cold War. Following Barre's ouster, Somalia descended into a lawless state. However, by 2005, the Islamic Courts Union (ICU) emerged as the principal power in Somalia. Covert U.S. activities in Somalia during 2005 may have led directly to the creation of Al Shabaab, which initially served as a militia to protect the ICU. The ICU is the parent of the terrorist organization Al Shabaab which, according the U.S. National Strategy for Counter Terrorism is presently the single greatest challenge to U.S. interests in the Horn of Africa. The U.S. successfully facilitated the destruction of the ICU in late 2006 to early 2007. However, Al Shabaab survived and adapted from being a militia to a guerrilla style terrorist organization. Had the U.S. remained engaged with Somalia continuously since the closing days of the Cold War, then it is possible that Somalia would not presently serve as the host to a major terrorist organization.

Taken as a whole, the two case studies in this project were designed to evaluate possible parallels between historical U.S. policy for Somalia against historical U.S policies for Iran and Afghanistan respectively. The bottom line is that although several parallels are present, the finalized analysis does not support a perfect linkage between the aforementioned policy approaches.

Figure 8.   Synthesis of Case Study Findings

Source: Created by author using data from tables 9 and 11.

Looking forward, the U.S. needs to leave no doubt that it is interested in seeing Somalia succeed and that it is willing to lead the effort. Somalia is important to the U.S. for five reasons: the nation is located in a strategically important location, serves as a haven to international piracy, is the origin of more than one million refugees, may be host to substantial hydro carbon reserves, and is the origin of the transnational terrorist organization Al Shabaab.

Somalis, and some elements in the international community at large, perceive the U.S. as being inconsistent in its interest with Somalia. The yo-yo of funding and interventionist techniques over the last three decades reveals a pattern of chasing shiny objects. The first shiny object being the perceived spread of communism (U.S. – Soviet Union proxy conflict in the Horn of Africa during the 1980s), the second shiny object being the desire to do good for struggling people but not sticking with it (UNITAF, UNISOM, UNISOM II and Operation Provide Relief missions), and the third shiny object was the elimination of anything that looked like a radical Islamic movement (destroying the ICU during the Government War on Terror, only to fan the flames of the less desirable Al Shabaab).

Failure on the part of the U.S. to be committed and consistent increases the chances of success for organizations like Al Shabaab. For those who view the interaction of nations as a zero-sum game, failure on the part of the U.S. to fully and consistently engage Somalia may open the window for countries like China or India to gain a stronger foothold in the region which in turn may jeopardize long term U.S. interests. Alternatively, the situation can be viewed as an opportunity for partnership between developed nations to improve the situation in Somalia in a permanent and sustained way. Consistent partnership over the long haul can certainly be viewed by many as superior to a meandering go-it-alone policy approach.

The conclusions portion of this chapter identifies that current counter insurgent strength is insufficient in Somalia. This finding is based on analysis of the current strategy being applied to deliver Somalia to a state of peace and prosperity. However, analysis indicates that a military solution is the incorrect solution for Al Shabaab. U.S. efforts to facilitate the demise of the ICU appear to have made matters worse, rather than better with respect to long term U.S. interests. Additionally, analysis indicates that Al Shabaab is unlikely to be defeated by military means. Religiously based terrorist organizations are far more likely to end due to some method of reconciliation (politization) or through policing. Rather than relying principally on the military instrument of national power, the U.S. and its partners should focus on diplomatic, information, and economic means to successfully achieve long term interests in Somalia.

BIBLIOGRAPHY

Books

Atwan, Abdel Bari. *After bin Laden: Al Qaeda, the next Generation*. New York: The New Press, 2012.

Baylis, John, James J. Wirtz, and Colin S. Gray. *Strategy in the Contemporary World: An Introduction to Strategic Studies.* 3rd ed. New York: Oxford University Press, 2010.

Bowden, Mark. *Black Hawk Down: A Story of Modern War*. New York: Penguin Books, 1999.

Burchill, Scott, ed. *Liberalism: Theories of International Relations*. 2nd ed. New York: Palgrave, 2001.

Call, Charles T., and Vanessa Wyeth. *Building States to Build Peace*. Boulder, CO: Lynne Rienner Publishers, 2008.

Coll, Steve. *Ghost Wars: The Secret History of the CIA, Afghanistan, and Bin Laden, from the Soviet Invasion to September 10, 2001.* New York: Penguin Press, 2004.

Crile, George. *Charlie Wilson's War*. New York: Grove Press, 2003.

Cronin, Audrey Kurth, *How Terrorism Ends*, Oxford: Princeton University Press, 2009.

De Waal, Alex. *Islamism and Its Enemies in the Horn of Africa*. Bloomington: Indiana University Press, 2004.

Easterly, William. *The White Man's Burden: Why the West's Efforts to Aid the Rest Have Done So Much Ill and So Little Good*. New York: Penguin, 2007.

Fisher, Sydney Nettleton, and William Ochsenwald. *The Middle East: A History Vol II*. New York: McGraw-Hill, 1997.

Galula, David. *Counterinsurgency Warfare; Theory and Practice*. Westport, CT: Praeger Security International, 1964.

Gasiorowski, Mark J., and Malcome Byrne. *Mohammad Mosaddeq and the 1953 Coup in Iran.* Syracuse, NY: Syracuse University Press, 2004.

Griswold, Eliza. *The Tenth Parallel: Dispatches from the Fault Line between Christianity and Islam.* New York: Macmillan, 2010.

Hansen, Stig Jarle. *Al-Shabaab in Somalia: The History and Ideology of a Militant Islamist Group.* London: C. Hurst and Company, 2013.

Jones, Seth G., and Martin C. Libicki, *How Terrorist Groups End: Lessons for Countering Al Qa'ida.* Santa Monica, CA: RAND Corporation, 2008.

Kinzer, Stephen. *All the Shah's Men, An American Coup and the Roots of Middle East Terror.* New York: John Wiley and Sons, 2003.

Kissinger, Hennery. *Diplomacy* New York: Simon and Schuster Inc., 1994.

Lippman, Thomas. *Understanding Islam; An Introduction to the Muslim World.* New York: The Penguin Group, 2002.

Menkhaus, Ken. *Somalia: State Collapse and the Threat of Terrorism.* London: Oxford University Press, 2004.

Phares, Walid. *The War of Ideas; Jihad Against Democracy.* New York: Palgrave Macmillan, 2007.

Pieterse, Jan Nederveen, *Development Theory.* 2nd ed. London: Sage Publications, 2010.

Pirio, Gregory A. *The African Jihad: Bin Laden's quest for the horn of Africa.* Trenton, NJ: The Red Sea Press, 2007.

Record, Reffery. *Beating Goliath; Why Insurgencies Win.* Washington, DC: Potomac Books Inc., 2007.

Ryan, David. *US Foreign Policy in World History; The New International History.* New York: Routledge, 2014.

Sachs, Jeffery D. *The End of Poverty: Economic Possibilities for Our Time.* New York: Penguin, 2006.

Westad, Odd Arne, *The Global Cold War.* New York: Cambridge University Press, 2005.

Government Documents

Office of the Coordinator for Counterterrorism. "Designation of al-Shabaab as a Specially Designated Global Terrorist." U.S. Department of State. 26 February 2008. http://www.state.gov/j/ct/rls/other/des/102448.htm (accessed 17 May 2014).

Office of the Press Secretary, "Notice – Continuation of the National Emergency with Respect to Somalia," The Whitehouse, 7 April 2014. http://www.whitehouse.gov/the-press-office/2014/04/07/notice-continuation-national-emergency-respect-somalia, (accessed 12 April 2014).

U.S. Army. Field Manual 3-24, *Counterinsurgency*. Washington, DC: Headquarters, Department of the Army, December 2006.

U.S. Government, Definitions of Terrorism in the U.S. Code. http://www.fbi.gov/about-us/investigate/terrorism/terrorism-definition (accessed 16 May 2014).

White House. *National Security Strategy of the United States.* Washington, DC: Whitehouse, 2010.

———. *National Strategy for Counterterrorism.* Washington, DC: Whitehouse, 2011.

Internet Sources

AllAfrica.com. "Somalia - Military in Deadly Battle With Police in Middle Shabelle." http://allafrica.com/stories/201404181389.html (accessed 1 May 2014).

Barack, Mohamed. "Mogadishu security declines as armed forces stretched outside capital." African Arguments. 16 April 2014. http://africanarguments.org/2014/04/16/mogadishu-security-declines-as-armed-forces-stretched-outside-capital-by-mohamed-mubarak/ (accessed 30 April 2014).

Drones Team. "Somalia: reported US covert actions 2001-2014." *The Bureau of Investigative Journalism.* 22 February 2012. http://www.thebureauinvestigates.com/2012/02/22/get-the-data-somalias-hidden-war/ (accessed 22 May 2014).

Farnesina. "Somalia: Italy's role for regional stability." 25 August 2010. http://www.esteri.it/MAE/EN/Sala_Stampa/ArchivioNotizie/Approfondimenti/2010/08/20100825_Somalia.htm (accessed 20 May 2014).

Federal Bureau of Investigation. "Police Employee Data." www2.fbi.gov/ucr/cius2009/police/ (accessed 1 May 2014).

Freedom House. "Somalia." http://www.freedomhouse.org/country/somalia#.U27q7PldUXs (accessed 10 February 2014).

Global Humanitarian Assistance. "International financing investments." 21 February 2012. http://www.globalhumanitarianassistance.org/wp-content/uploads/2012/02/gha-somalia-briefing-paper-feb-2012-final.pdf (accessed 20 April 2014).

Governing.com. "Law Enforcement Officers Per Capita for Cities, Local Departments." www.governing.com/gov-data/safety-justice/law-enforcement-police-department-employee-totals-for-cities.html (accessed 1 May 2014).

IMF. "IMF Recognizes the Federal Government of Somalia After 22-year Interval." 12 April 2013. https://www.imf.org/external/np/sec/pr/2013/pr13119.htm (accessed 22 May 2014).

Kalif. "America's interests in Somalia: Four major U.S. oil companies are sitting on a prospective fortune in exclusive concessions." Global Research. 3 January 2007. http://www.globalresearch.ca/america-s-interests-in-somalia-four-major-u-s-oil-companies-are-sitting-on-a-prospective-fortune-in-exclusive-concessions/4342 (accessed 20 April 2014).

Kelly, Michael. "US Special Ops Have Become Much, Much Scarier Since 9/11." *Business Insider.* 10 May 2013. http://www.businessinsider.com/the-rise-of-jsoc-in-dirty-wars-2013-4 (accessed 20 May 2014).

Masters, Jonathan, and Zachary Laub. "Hezbollah." Council on Foreign Relations. 3 January 2014. http://www.cfr.org/lebanon/hezbollah-k-hizbollah-hizbullah/p9155 (accessed on 22 May 2014).

The National Counterterrorism Center. "Hizballah." http://www.nctc.gov/site/groups/hizballah.html (accessed 22 May 2014).

Office of the Historian. "Kennan and Containment." U.S. Department of State. http://history.state.gov/milestones/1945-1952/kennan (accessed 19 May 2014).

————. "NSC 68, 1950." U.S. Department of State. http://history.state.gov/milestones/1945-1952/NSC68 (accessed 15 February 2014).

Osman, Ahmed. "Somalia's Fractures Getting Hard to Heal." *Inter Press News Agency.* 6 September 2013. http://www.ipsnews.net/2013/09/somalias-fractures-getting-hard-to-heal/ (accessed 15 November 2013).

Pike, John. "Hizballah, "Party of God, Islamic Jihad, Islamic Jihad for the Liberation of Palestine, Organization of the Oppressed on Earth, Revolutionary Justice Organization."" *Federation of American Scientists.* 18 March 2005. http://www.fas.org/irp/world/para/hizballah.htm (accessed 21 May 2014).

Richardson, Josh. "The Somali Diaspora: A Key Counterterrorism Ally." https://www.ctc.usma.edu/posts/the-somali-diaspora-a-key-counterterrorism-ally (accessed 15 April 2014).

Sabahi. "700 Somali soldiers fired for incompetence." 5 February 2014. http://sabahionline.com/en_GB/articles/hoa/articles/newsbriefs/2014/02/05/newsbrief-04 (accessed 15 March 2014).

Schippert, Steve. "al-Qaeda and the ICU's Somali Retreat." Threats Watch. 2 January 2007. http://threatswatch.org/inbrief/2007/01/alqaeda-and-the-icus-somali-re/ (accessed 19 May 2014).

Seid, Mohammed Mealin. "The Role of Religion In The Ogaden Conflict." *Social Science Research Council.* 26 January 2009. http://hornofafrica.ssrc.org/mealin/printable.html (accessed 15 April 2014).

United Nations Department of Field Support. "Map of Somalia." December 2011. http://www.un.org/depts/Cartographic/map/profile/ somalia.pdf (accessed 2 May 2014).

United Nations Office for the Coordination of Humanitarian Affairs. "Major Donors of Humanitarian Assistance to Somalia in 1996/1997. 28 July 1998. http://fts.unocha.org/arfts/1997/som9697/som96-71.html (accessed 10 January 2014).

Wood, Josh. "Hezbollah Rolls The Dice in Syria." *Aljazeera America.* 10 September 2013. http://america.aljazeera.com/articles/2013/9/10/hezbollah-rolls-thediceinsyria.html (accessed 20 May 2014).

The World Bank. "Afghanistan–World Development Indicators." http://data.worldbank.org/country/Afghanistan (accessed 15 May 2014).

———. "Iran." http://data.worldbank.org/country/iran-islamic-republic (accessed 20 May 2014).

———. "Lebanon." http://data.worldbank.org/country/Lebanon (accessed 20 May 2014).

———. "Somalia–World Development Indicators." http://data.worldbank.org/ country/somalia (accessed 1 March 2014).

Journals/Periodicals

Bilmes, Linda J. and Michael D. Intriligator. "How Many Wars Is the US Fighting Today?" *Peace Economic, Peace Science, and Public Policy* 19, no. 1 (2013): 10.

Burgess, Stephen F. "Stabilization, Peacebuilding, and Sustainability in the Horn of Africa." *Strategic Studies Quarterly* (Spring 2009): 81-118.

Kennan, George F. ("X"). "The Sources of Soviet Conduct." *Foreign Affairs* 25, no. 4, (July 1947): 566-582.

"Somalia Breaks with Soviet Union, Cuba: The Somalia Story: A year of Diplomatic Warfare." *Executive Intelligence Review* 4, no. 47, (22 November 1977): 54.

Newspapers

Cowell, N. Alan. "Guerrilla Drive in Somalia seen as part of a Proxy War." *The New York Times*, 16 July 1982.

Dehghan, Saeed Kamali and Richard Norton-Taylor. "CIA Admits Role in 1953 Iranian Coup." *The Guardian,* 19 August 2013.

Fineman, Mark. "The Oil Factor in Somalia." *Los Angeles Times*, 18 January 1993.

Kelly, Tom, and Tim Shipman. "Foreign aid to Somalia 'helps Al Qaeda': Pressure grows to divert cash back to the UK." *Mail*, 23 February 2014.

Mazzetti, Mark. "Efforts by CIA Fail in Somalia, Officials Charge." *The New York Times*, 8 June 2006.

Nakhoul, Samia. "Analysis: Hezbollah tips Syria power balance, polarizes Lebanon." *Reuters*, 11 June 2013.

Naylor, Sean D. "The Secret War: Africa Ops May Be Just Starting." *The Army Times*, 5 December 2011.

Ngugi, Mukoma Wa. "How al-Shabaab was born." *The Guardian*, 4 October 2013.

Nichols, Michelle, and Louis Charbonneau. "Exclusive: Western oil exploration in Somalia may spark conflict – U.N. report." *Chicago Tribune*, 17 July 2013.

Perlez, Jane. "Bush Sees Victims of Somali Famine." *The New York Times*, 1 January 1993.

Salad, Hamdi. "Somali Minister of Defence: Government committed to re-building army." *Sabahi*, 25 March 2014.

Scahill, Jeremy. "The CIA's Secret Sites in Somalia." *The Nation*, 12 July 2012.

Smith, David. "Al-Shabaab rebuilds forces in Somalia as African Union campaign stalls." *The Guardian*, 28 October 2013.

Talbot, Chris. "US Continues Covert Action In Somalia." *The Somaliland Times*, 27 September 2006.

Wax, Emily, and Karen DeYoung. "U.S. Secretly Backing Warlords in Somalia." *Washington Post,* 17 May 2006.

Witaker, Brian. "The definition of terrorism." *The Guardian*, 7 May 2001.

Young, Sarah. "Somalia favours firms with pre-1991 deals for oil exploration." *Reuters*; 2 October 2012.

Reports

Barnes, Cedric and Harun Hassan. *The Rise and Fall of Mogadishu's Islamic Courts.* London: Chatham House, 2007.

Blanchard, Christopher M. *The Islamic Traditions of Wahhabism and Salafiyya.* Washington DC: CRS Report for Congress, 2007.

Cuevas, Eloy E., and Madeleine Wells. *Somalia: Line in the Sand – Identification of MYM Vulnerabilities*. Carlisle, PA: U.S. Army War College, 2011.

Dagne, Ted. *Somalia: Current Conditions and Prospects for a Lasting Peace*. Washington, DC: CRS Report for Congress, 2011.

Jones, Seth G. *The Terrorist Threat from Al Shabaab*. Santa Monica, CA: RAND Corporation, 2013.

Pailthorp, Melissa C. *Development before Disaster: USAID in Somalia 1978-1990*. Washington, DC: Report for USAID, 1994.

Patman, Robert G. *Strategic Shortfall: The Somalia Syndrome and the March to 9/11*. Santa Barbara: ABC-CLIO, 2010.

Ploch, Lauren. *Countering Terrorism in East Africa: The U.S. Response*. Washington, DC: CRS Report for Congress, 2010.

Ploch-Blanchard, Lauren. *The September 2013 Terrorist Attack in Kenya: In Brief*. Washington DC: CRS Report for Congress, 2013.

U.N. Office for the Coordination of Humanitarian Affairs. *Common Humanitarian Fund for Somalia: Revised First Standard Allocation 2013–April/May 2013*. New York: OCHA, 2013.

————. *Consolidated Annual Financial Report on Activities Implemented under the Somalia Common Humanitarian Fund: Report of the Administrative Agent of the Somalia CHF for the period 1 January – 31 December 2011*. New York: OCHA, 2012.

————. *Somalia Common Humanitarian Fund–Annual Report 2012*. New York: OCHA, 2012.

U.N. Security Council; *Report of the Monitoring Group on Somalia and Eritrea pursuant to Security Council resolution 2060 (2012): Somalia*. New York: United Nations, 12 July 2013.

U.S. General Accounting Office. *Peace Operations: U.S. Costs in Support of Haiti, Former Yugoslavia, Somalia, and Rwanda*. Washington, DC: GAO, 1996.

USAID. *FY 2003 Performance and Accountability Report*. Washington, DC: USAID, 2003.

————. *Somalia–Complex Emergency: Fact Sheet #1, Fiscal Year (FY) 2013*. Washington, DC: USAID, 2013.

———. *Where Does USAID's Money Go?* Washington, DC: USAID, 30 September 2012.

Weiss, Kenneth. "The Soviet Involvement in the Ogaden War." Professional Paper 269, Center for Naval Analyses, 1980.